THE
Walker's
COMPANION

Edited by Malcolm Tait

THE RAMBLERS' ASSOCIATION

*A journey of a thousand miles
begins with a single step*

A very well-known proverb

THINK
BOOKS

A Think Book

First published in 2003 by Think Publishing

Think Publishing
The Pall Mall Deposit
124-128 Barlby Road
London W10 6BL

Tel: 020 8962 3020
Fax: 020 8962 8689

www.thinkpublishing.co.uk

Editor: Malcolm Tait
The Companion team: Vicky Bamforth, James Collins, Rhiannon Guy,
Annabel Holmes, Louise Tait and Olive Tayler
Cover illustration: Thomas Boivin

© Think Publishing 2003

Researched and compiled by Think Publishing
Printed and bound by William Clowes
Distribution by Airlift Book Company

The Ramblers' Association
2nd Floor, Camelford House,
87-90 Albert Embankment, London SE1 7TW
www.ramblers.org.uk
Tel: 020 7339 8500

Papers supplied by William Clowes are natural, renewable and recyclable
products. They are made from wood grown in sustainable forests. The
logging and manufacturing processes conform to the environmental
regulations of the country of origin.

ISBN 0-9541363-4-9

*The walker's companions are
the stones in his boot,
the rain in his face,
the unreadable map...
...but a wide open space*

A much less well-known proverb

THINK
BOOKS

A BIG-BOOTED, STEPPIN'-OUT, HIGH-KICKIN' THANK YOU

This book would not have been possible without the research, ideas, and dogged support of:

Sheila Adams, Colin Antwis, Claire Ashton, Laure Baudon, Clare Benians, Jo Bourne, Rachael Bryett, Simon Calder, Gwen Campbell, Lindsay Crawford, Des de Moor, Emily Elgar, Jacquetta Fewster, Dan French, Doreen Gathercole, Ian Gillett, Elaine Hilditch, Dani Ismail, Eric Kenyon, Gill Learner, Nigel Millward, Nick Milton, Ade Morris, D R Pow, Emily Richmond, Norman W Smith, Roly Smith, Katie Spencer-Smith, Natalie Sternberg, Tristan Stubbs, W Sutcliffe, Peter Tait, Paul Wilkinson, Charlotte Williams, Jamie Winslow, Patricia Wright, and the staff at the Ramblers' Association.

Most introductions explain what the book is. Let's be different. Let's start by explaining what it's not.

The Walker's Companion is NOT a guide, it tells you NOTHING about accommodation and equipment stores, and it most certainly WON'T show you how to get from A to B or any other letter. If you're looking for information on walking around Britain and making use of its facilities as you go, then the Ramblers' Association already publishes a nifty little yearbook and accommodation guide that should see you right.

But wherever you walk, *The Walker's Companion* will have something for you. Whether you're cradling your pint at the end of a long trek, or just nursing your tootsies having come back from the shops, this is the book that you'll want to have close at hand.

Because when you're at rest you'll want to find out the true walking facts of life. How many feet does a centipede REALLY have? How long it would take you to walk to the moon, and how can you learn how to walk on your hands? Why are they called Pelican crossings, and how do thermos flasks actually work? And what on earth, anyway, is psychrotentiginosity...?

Just think of the relief you'll feel as you delve into *The Walker's Companion*, the only book with all the answers to the REAL walking questions of today.

Malcolm Tait, Editor, November 2003

Your easy at-a-glance calculation of shoe size

Length Ins	Length Cms	UK size	EU size	US size
1.67	4.23		6	
2.00	5.08		8	
2.33	5.93		9	
2.67	6.77		10	
3.00	7.62		11	0
3.33	8.47		13	0.5
3.67	9.31		14	1
4.00	10.16	0	15	1.5
4.33	11.01	1	17	2.5
4.67	11.85	2	18	3.5
5.00	12.70	3	19	4.5
5.33	13.55	4	20	5.5
5.67	14.39	5	22	6.5
6.00	15.24	6	23	7.5
6.33	16.09	7	24	8.5
6.67	16.93	8	25	9.5
7.00	17.78	9	27	10.5
7.33	18.63	10	28	11.5
7.67	19.47	11	29	12.5
8.00	20.32	12	30	13.5
8.33	21.17	13	32	14.5
8.67	22.01	1	33	2.5
9.00	22.86	2	34	3.5
9.33	23.71	3	36	4.5
9.67	24.55	4	37	5.5
10.00	25.40	5	38	6.5
10.33	26.25	6	39	7.5
10.67	27.09	7	41	8.5
11.00	27.94	8	42	9.5
11.33	28.79	9	43	10.5
11.67	29.63	10	44	11.5
12.00	30.48	11	46	12.5
12.33	31.33	12	47	13.5
12.67	32.17	13	48	14.5
13.00	33.02	14	50	15.5
13.33	33.87	15	51	16.5
13.67	34.71	16	52	17.5
14.00	35.56	17	53	18.5
14.33	36.41	18	55	19.5
14.67	37.25	19	56	20.5
15.00	38.10	20	57	21.5
15.33	38.95	21	58	22.5
15.67	39.79	22	60	23.5

RAMBLING RIDDLE

How far can a 7-foot tall man walk into a forest?
Answer on page 153.

MAD FOR WALKING

Colonial Jack left Portland, Maine, on June 1st 1908, on an attempt to walk around the border of the USA, all the while pushing a wheelbarrow. The journey measured 9,000 miles in total; it was Jack's aim to complete the odyssey in 400 days (not including Sundays), covering an average of 22.5 miles per day. Starting from Portland, Maine, he walked along the Canadian border to Seattle, Washington, descended the Pacific coast to Los Angeles, California, crossed the southern border and coastline to Jacksonville, in Florida, and finally returned to Portland along the Atlantic coast. He finished the walk in 357 days, 43 days ahead of time, averaging over 25 miles per day. Colonial Jack is rightly remembered as having accomplished one of the greatest walking feats in history.

QUOTE UNQUOTE

Walk and be happy, walk and be healthy. The best way to lengthen out our days is to walk steadily and with a purpose.
CHARLES DICKENS, novelist

12 FILMS THAT THOSE WHO WALK MIGHT WANT TO CATCH

A Walk to Remember 2002

A Walk in the Sun 1945

Walk 1999, then in 2002 and 2003

Walk Don't Run 1966

Walk a Crooked Mile 1948

The Walk 1991 and again in 2001

Walk on the Wild Side 1962

Walk Tall 1960

Rabbit-proof Fence 2002 (aka *Long Walk Home*)

Cake Walk 1898

Long Walk to Freedom 2004

The Lambeth Walk 1940 (aka *Me and My Girl*)

Graham failed to notice the tell-tale stain he had left in the snow

MODERN PILGRIMAGES

Diana, Princess of Wales, is buried on an island in an ornamental lake in Althorp Park. Althorp House, her family's home for over five centuries, is set in 15,000 acres of Northamptonshire countryside and stands just a mile away. An ancient arboretum stands nearby, which contains trees planted by Prince William and Prince Harry, other members of her family and the princess herself.

The length, in inches, of the Yeti footprint in the 1951 photograph taken near Mount Everest   13

SEXUAL PLEASURES THAT
WALKERS MIGHT ENJOY

Agoraphilia is arousal from having sex in public places. People who enjoy having sex in a public park, field or other exposed area get their thrill from the possibility of being discovered. The line between agoraphilia and agoraphobia – a fear of open spaces – can be a very fine one.

WALKER CUP WINNERS SINCE
THE LAST DRAW

The Walker Cup is an amateur golf tournament between the United States, and Great Britain and Ireland.

1965 Draw, 12-12
1967 United States, 15-9
1969 United States, 13-11
1971 Britain-Ireland, 13-11
1973 United States, 14-10
1975 United States, 15-8
1977 United States, 16-8
1979 United States, 15-8
1981 United States, 15-9
1983 United States, 13-10

1985 United States, 13-11
1987 United States, 16-7
1989 Britain-Ireland, 12-11
1991 United States, 14-10
1993 United States, 19-5
1995 Britain-Ireland, 14-10
1997 United States, 18-6
1999 Britain-Ireland, 15-9
2001 Britain-Ireland, 15-9
2003 Britain-Ireland, 12-11

LOOKED GOOD ON PAPER

Neither Tom Stephenson, the man who came up with the idea of the Pennine Way, nor Alfred Wainwright, who wrote an early guidebook to Britain's first long-distance path, ever walked the entire 270-mile route in one outing.

WALKING WORDS

Once trodden by human feet, a natural path becomes a work of man, each traveller marking the way for the next, sometimes departing from the most direct or obvious route to avoid a muddy patch, or to keep out of sight of possible enemies. Feet follow footsteps, and so a road is trodden into history.

The Oldest Road, An Exploration of the Ridgeway,
JRL Anderson and Fay Godwin

It is the bright day that brings forth the adder,
And that craves wary walking.
WILLIAM SHAKESPEARE, Julius Caesar

EAT MY SHOES

When ballerina Marie Taglioni danced her final ballet in Russia in 1842, a group of St Petersburg fans cobbled together 200 roubles for her dancing slippers, cooked them up and ate them with a special sauce.

Werner Herzog eats his Shoe is a 22-minute film of the German film director... eating his shoe. Werner Herzog unwisely told his student Errol Morris that if a successful documentary on pet cemeteries was ever made he would eat his shoe. When Morris presented the film, Herzog fulfilled his promise. He sautéed his shoe in a broth of garlic and spices and ate it in front of an audience, where it was, predictably, filmed.

CNN broadcaster Tucker Carlson vowed to eat his shoes if Hillary Clinton's published memoir *Living History* sold more than one million copies. On hearing of her success he vowed to keep to his word adding 'I'm going for slip-ons, nothing with laces'. A number of Manhattan chefs offered to cook them up for him and suggestions included deep-fried sole and lace linguine, sweat and sour sauce and Tiramishoe.

In *The Gold Rush* Charlie Chaplin plays a lone prospector who travels to Alaska to dig for gold. On Thanksgiving he was forced – from starvation – to boil and eat his boot. Chaplin simmered it as if he was producing a five-star feast, carving and filleting it and then pouring on a watery gravy. He treated the sole as a delicacy, twirled the laces like spaghetti and sucked the nails as if they were chicken bones. Everyone laughed.

In 1996 installation artist Yu Xiuzhen staged an exhibition in Tibet which included pairs of shoes arranged all over a hill, each one filled with butter.

WEATHER LORE FOR WALKERS

Rain before seven;
Fine before eleven

Generally, a given area is unlikely to experience rain from a low-pressure system for long periods, and rainfall that starts the previous evening will probably cease before noon.

BARE FACTS

Walkers lost the right to walk through a route in Cumbria when a local authority settled a dispute in 2002. Why? Since 1972, the route has passed through a nudist camp. The nudists successfully campaigned for their right to privacy to be respected, ending the 30-year war of words between naturist and naturalist.

WALKING DREAMS

Ramble
To dream that you are rambling through the country denotes that you will be oppressed with sadness and separation from friends, but your worldly surroundings will be all that one could desire. For a young woman, this dream promises a comfortable home, but early bereavement.

Walking
To dream of walking through rough briar-entangled paths denotes that you will be much distressed over your business complications, and disagreeable misunderstandings will produce coldness and indifference. To walk in pleasant places means you will be the possessor of fortune and favour. To walk in the night brings misadventure and unavailing struggle for contentment. For a young woman to find herself walking rapidly in her dreams denotes that she will inherit some property, and will possess a much desired object.

Walking Stick
To see a walking stick in a dream foretells that you will enter into contracts without proper deliberation, and will consequently suffer reverses. If you use one in walking, you will be dependent upon the advice of others. To admire handsome ones, you will entrust your interests to others, but they will be faithful.

Climbing
To dream of climbing up a hill or mountain and reaching the top, you will overcome the most formidable obstacles between you and a prosperous future; but if you should fail to reach the top, your dearest plans will suffer being wrecked.

Interpretations by dream specialist Gustavus Miller, 1901

HIGH SOCIETY

The high heel was first developed by Mongol tribesmen who wore bright red wooden heels when riding. Their style was so perfect that it gained respect within European society and was adopted as fashion.

WATER WALKS

ST. MICHAEL'S MOUNT, CORNWALL

Formerly a monastery, the Mount's castle – the most famous of Cornwall's landmarks – dates from the 14th century. The island is steeped in folklore: one legend tells of a local lad who slayed its incumbent giant.

The South West Coast Path runs through Penzance and continues for three miles along the coast to Marazion, but it is also possible to walk along the beach at low tide. Mount's Bay is one of the most beautiful in the world, with stunning views of the Mount.

Access to the island is on foot across the causeway at low tide, or by ferry at high tide.

WALKING WORDS

Travel does not merely broaden the mind. It makes the mind. Our early explorations are the raw materials of our intelligence…Children need paths to explore, to take bearings on the earth in which they live, as a navigator takes the bearings on familiar landmarks. If we excavate the memories of childhood, we remember the paths first, things and people second – paths down the garden, the way to school, the way round the house, corridors through the bracken or long grass. Tracking the paths of animals was the first and most important element in the education of early man.

With Chatwin: Portrait of a Writer, Susannah Clapp

MAD FOR WALKING

Emma Gatewood lived for most of her life on a farm, where she raised 11 children and four grandchildren, worked her fields, and planted flower and vegetable gardens. Her life changed at age 71, when, after seeing a *National Geographic* article about the Appalachian Trail and discovering that no woman had ever hiked the entire length, Grandma Gatewood began her adventure. Her first attempt ended soon after she had started when she broke her spectacles and was forced to return home. In 1958, however, she successfully hiked the complete length of the trail from Maine to Georgia, only to repeat her achievement in 1960 and again in 1963. Grandma never brought with her the expensive paraphernalia so beloved of the modern hiker. She would always travel light, merely carrying a blanket, plastic sheet, cup, first aid kit, raincoat, and a change of clothes. Instead of walking boots, she chose an old pair of tennis shoes. And there were no freeze-dried meals for her. Her meals consisted of dried beef, cheese and nuts, accompanied by any food that she might find along the path. Fans have ensured that her achievement is remembered by naming part of the Appalachian after her.

SEXUAL PLEASURES THAT
WALKERS MIGHT ENJOY

Foot tickling is an age-old erotic stimulus and known worldwide. Paintings of foot tickling can be seen in the Louvre as well as in the Museum of Pius Clementia in Rome. They are also found in China, Japan, India and Southeast Asia.

Queen Hatshepsut used to prepare for her lovers with exquisite pod-cosmetic care. The skin of her feet would be rubbed and scented with oil and palace eunuchs would tickle the bottoms of her feet with peacock feathers to bring her to a pitch of sexual readiness. The noble and aristocratic Russians, too, were devotees of sexual foot tickling.

Foot tickling for sexual arousal was used in the Muscovite palaces and courts for centuries. Many of the Czarinas were fervent participants. When their feet were gently stroked, many women experienced intense erotic pleasure. The practice was so popular that eunuchs and women were employed as full time foot ticklers. This unique skill was developed so well that their occupations brought prestige and good pay. Anna Leopoldovna had at least six ticklers at her feet. While the ticklers performed their task, they also told saucy stories and sang obscene ballads. This was done to work the ladies up to an erotic pitch so that they could meet their husbands or lovers in a sexually impassioned mood.

GREAT MOMENTS IN THE
HISTORY OF FOOTWEAR

Sandals originated in warm climates where the soles of the feet needed protection but the top of the foot needed to be cool.

4,000 years ago the first shoes were made of a single piece of rawhide that enveloped the foot for both warmth and protection.

In Europe pointed toes on shoes were fashionable from the eleventh to the fifteenth centuries.

In the Middle East heels were added to shoes to lift the foot from the burning sand.

In Europe in the sixteenth and seventeenth centuries heels on shoes were always coloured red.

Shoes all over the world were identical until the nineteenth century, when left and right-footed shoes were first made in Philadelphia.

Six-inch-high heels were worn by the upper classes in seventeenth-century Europe. Two servants, one on either side, were needed to hold up the person wearing the high heels.

Sneakers were first made in America in 1916. They were originally called keds.

The first lady's boot was designed for Queen Victoria in 1840.

TEN THINGS SLEEPWALKERS HAVE DONE

Ridden a horse • Made breakfast • Stripped wallpaper
Repaired a fridge • Jumped out of a window • Had sex while still
snoring • Eaten buttered cigarettes • Eaten cat food sandwiches •
Eaten raw bacon • Eaten their watch

MAD FOR WALKING

For more than 30 years, Arthur Blessitt has carried a 12-foot, 40-pound cross around the world, and travelled a total of 36,067 miles on foot. This is the first time that a cross has been carried around the world, and his journey has become the longest ever.

Blessitt has crossed seven continents, wearing down a pair of shoes every five hundred miles; his longest walk in a day was 71 miles in 24 hours. He has taken the cross to 296 countries, been arrested 24 times, and been welcomed warmly by both the Israeli Army and the Palestinian Liberation Army. He has witnessed wars in 50 countries, including those in the Lebanon and in Mozambique. Blessitt's favourite city was Jerusalem, while the coldest temperature he has experienced was in Nova Scotia in Canada.

The cross has been lost, stolen, broken and dropped overboard, while Blessitt has been attacked by crocodiles and baboons, and chased by elephants. He faced a firing squad in Nicaragua, a stoning in Morocco, and a pistol attack in Florida.

Blessitt notes that the cross has been refused overnight stays at more than half the churches requested, but he has never been turned away from leaving it overnight at a bar or nightclub in his walks around the world.

FARES AND WAYFARERS

A common London practice was, and still is, to take a train to a more rural destination, follow a walking route, and return home from a different station. These are some examples of the Great Western Railway's Walking Tour tickets from Paddington Station in 1928.

Tour No.	Outward by Rail to	Distance of walk in miles	Returning same day by rail from	Return Fares 1st	2nd
1	Northolt Halt	7	West Drayton	2s 4d	1s 5d
2	Northolt Junction	5	West Drayton	2s 4d	1s 5d
3	Ruislip & Ickenham	7.5	Gerrards Cross	3s 7d	2s 2d
4	Denham	15	Staines	3s 2d	2s 2d
5	Gerrards Cross	6	Slough	3s 11d	2s 4d
6	Beaconsfield	16.5	Twyford	6s 6d	3s 11d

RAMBLING RIDDLE

The riddle asked of Oedipus by the Sphinx:
I walk on four legs in the morning, two legs at noon, three legs in the
evening. What am I? Answer on page 153.

SHOEMAKERS' HEROES

St. Crispin is the patron saint of shoemakers. Since medieval times, October 25th has been celebrated as St. Crispin's Day and the Shoemaker's Holiday.

In the past, boot and shoemakers traditionally closed their shops on this day, in celebration and commemoration.

St. Crispin was born into a wealthy Roman family in the third century A.D. Somewhere fairly early on, he converted to Christianity. Since this was not an approved lifestyle for a noble Roman, legend says that he was disinherited. Forced to fall back upon his own resources, St. Crispin (not yet a saint) became a shoemaker. Although teaching the gospel was his life's work, he made shoes in his spare time – until he was put to death for his beliefs in Soissons, France in 288 A.D.

We know a little more about St. Hugh, the English counterpart to St. Crispin. Born Hugh, son of Arviragus – king of Powisland (part of modern day Wales), St. Hugh married a Christian princess, Winifred of Flintshire. She quickly converted him to Christianity, with roughly the same results. Thrown into poverty, Hugh became a shoemaker who preached the gospel by day and plied his craft by night. Both he and Winifred were put to death, ostensibly for rabble-rousing, about 300 A.D. Legend has it that his fellow shoemakers kept constant vigil and consoled him during the time of his internment. After his death, by hanging, his friends pulled his body from the gibbet and dried his bones. These were made into tools for making shoes. For many years, in fact, a shoemaker's tool kit was called St. Hugh's Bones.

QUOTE UNQUOTE

I wish I loved the human race
I wish I loved its silly face
I wish I liked the way it walks
I wish I liked the way it talks
And when I'm introduced to one
I wish I thought 'What jolly fun'.
SIR WALTER A RALEIGH, Laughter from a Cloud

Number of pounds raised by first UK charity walk (1959, for World Refugee Fund)

Many long distance paths have imaginative waymarkers designed to prevent ramblers from wandering off the trail.

The Donnington Way Top of the list has to be this marker, simply featuring an enticing mug of frothy ale. The sign speaks for itself – thirsty walkers would be well advised to follow this route through rural Gloucestershire that links the 15 pubs of the Donnington Brewery. Starting in Stow-on-the-Wold, the path ends 62 miles later in the same town.

Boudicca's Way Ramblers following this path, named after the legendary warrior queen of the Iceni, need to look out for the sword that appears on its waymarkers. The route covers 40 miles between Norwich and Diss in Norfolk, through lands formerly inhabited by the Celtic tribes of the East of England.

The Bunyan Trail A silhouetted profile of John Bunyan, author of The Pilgrim's Progress, distinguishes this trail from others in the Bedfordshire area. The circular route begins in the Sundon Hills Country Park and wends through Elstow, taking in places of interest connected with Bunyan.

The Bonnie Prince Charlie Walk Waymarkers dotted along this Derbyshire walk feature the profile of Prince Charles Edward Stuart, or Bonnie Prince Charlie, and the legend '1745-1945'. Its route begins in Ashbourne and ends in Derby, following the Prince's 1745 march between the two towns. The path was created 250 years later to commemorate the 60th anniversary of the founding of the Ramblers' Association.

The Jurassic Way Those walking along this path can be assured that huge primordial reptilians are not often sighted in rural Oxfordshire and Northamptonshire. Its name in fact derives from the Jurassic rocks (of between 140 and 195 million years old) that lie beneath the countryside between Banbury and Stamford; the shell motif on its waymarkers hints at the fossil treasures below.

The walk's route is considered to follow a prehistoric pathway running along a watershed created by ancient limestone escarpments.

WALKING AND BRAS

The Playtex moonwalk is an annual event organised by women around the world who power walk marathons in their bras in aid of breast cancer charities. In the UK it takes place at night, starting and finishing in Battersea Park and in 2003 it raised £3,391,333.

WEATHER LORE FOR WALKERS

Beware the oak, it draws the stroke.
Avoid an ash, it courts the flash.
Creep under the thorn. It will save you from harm.

A German study in 1900 found that one beech would be struck to six spruce, 37 pine and 60 oaks. An English study in 1935 found that 13 poplar were struck against 26 ash, 32 elm and 61 oaks. Tall trees in open ground, on woodland borders and on sandy soil are more likely to be struck; smooth-barked trees are less of a risk than rough barked species, like the deadly oak.

QUOTE UNQUOTE

The body's habituation to walking as normal stems from the good old days. It was the bourgeois form of locomotion: physical demythologization, free of the spell of hieratic pacing, roofless wandering, breathless flight. Human dignity insisted on the right to walk, a rhythm not extorted from the body by command or terror. The walk, the stroll, were private ways of passing time, the heritage of the feudal promenade in the nineteenth century.
THEODOR W ADORNO, philosopher

A FEW ORDNANCE SURVEY MARKERS

Flush brackets: Flush brackets are metal plates cemented onto the fronts of buildings and on triangulation pillars. In fact a type of bench mark, they are spaced at intervals of approximately 1.5km from each other. The number visible on each bracket is simply a serial number, and does not give its height above sea level.

Bench marks: Usually found on buildings (especially churches), these marks consist of a horizontal line with an arrow pointing up to it from below. Cut by Ordnance Survey levelling staff, they were used to give a network of points from which the height above sea level was precisely measured. There were formerly around half a million of these marks on buildings throughout Great Britain; however new mapping techniques have rendered them unnecessary, and around half have disappeared.

Fundamental bench marks: With deep foundations, buried chambers and granite pillars, fundamental bench marks are very stable alternatives to the other two markers. They are positioned far apart from each other, at distances of 40km.

He was a peasant, but he was a rambler also... He loved winter as he did the mountains, and probably the sea in the same way, though the Muse did claim to have seen him 'seek the sounding shore, delighted with the dashing roar'. She said, too, that she had seen him struck by 'Nature's visage hoar' under the north wind, and he has told us himself that 'There is scarcely any earthly object gives me more – I don't know if I should call it pleasure, but something which exalts me, something which enraptures me – than to walk in the sheltered side of a wood or high plantation, in a cloudy winter day, and hear a stormy wind howling among the trees and raving o'er the plain.'

A Literary Pilgrim in England, **Edward Thomas**
On Robert Burns. Unsurprisingly, this is from a chapter on Scotland.

THE GIRAFFE AND THE ELEPHANT
WENT FOR A WALK

The giraffe and the elephant went for a walk.
They stopped in some shade and started to talk;
'I wish it would rain,' said the giraffe with a sigh.
'I'm tired of watching the clouds pass us by!'
'Yes,' said the elephant, 'Where is the rain?
I wish I could eat fresh green leaves again.
The sun is so hot and the land is so dry;
When will the rain fall from the sky?'
Later in the day the sky turned grey,
The flying ants flew out to say,
'The rain is coming! We smell it in the air!
And in the distance, thunder we hear!'
The giraffe and the elephant looked up at the sky
And heard the black eagle give forth his cry,
'The rain has come, The rivers will flow;
The dry season is over; now the green grass will grow!'
A Zulu song

WALK LIKE AN ANIMAL

Basilisk lizards are part of the iguana family. They have the nickname 'Jesus Christ Lizard' because when fleeing from a predator, they can run on top of the water. Basilisks actually have large hind feet with flaps of skin between each toe. The fact that they move quickly across the water, aided by their web-like feet, gives them the appearance of walking on water. Smaller basilisks can run about 10-20 metres on the water without sinking. Young basilisks can usually run further than older ones. They dwell in Central and South American rainforests.

A FEW WALKING DATES

4 million years BC
Australopithecus afarensis begins the habit of two-legged walking, the diagnostic skill of the family Hominidae.

10,000–8,000 years BC
North Americans begin to make and wear sandals.

100 AD
Emperor Hadrian tours his whole empire on foot, marching 21 miles a day in full armour.

1589
Sir Robert Carey walks 300 miles from London to Berwick for a bet.

1801–1803
Johann Gottfried Seume walks from Germany to Sicily and back, then takes another trip from Germany to Russia, Finland and Sweden from 1805–1807.

1809
Captain Robert Barclay walks 1,000 miles in 1,000 hours, up and down a measured mile at Newmarket Heath.

1864
Formation of the Black Forest Wanderverein. It is today the world's oldest surviving walking club.

1860-1903
The Pedestrian Age is ushered in, with walking becoming the leading sport in the western world.

1861
Edward Payson Weston bets that President Lincoln will lose the 1860 election. Upon Lincon's win and Weston's loss, Weston walks from Boston to the inauguration in Washington DC.

1935
Formation of the Ramblers' Association, now with 141,000 members.

1969
Neil Armstrong and Buzz Aldrin walk on moon.

1999/2000: Millennium Walks and World Walking Day Walks held worldwide.

SCAPA FLOW FOR A BALL OF CHALK

Decided to Scapa Flow for a ball of chalk. Looked out the burnt cinder: no Andy Cain. Put on my daisy roots and went out on my Jack Jones, down the frog and toad until I reached a field of April showers. The Richard the Thirds were in full ding dong in the currant bun, but no bow and arrows. Came back along the main field of wheat, popped into the rub-a-dub to rest my plates of meat, then home in time for Jim Skinner. *Translation: The missing words are: Alone, Birds, Boots, Dinner, Feet, Flowers, Go, Pub, Rain, Road, Song, Sparrows, Street, Sun, Walk, Window. Although not in that order.*

24   *Date in April 1932 of the Battle of Kinder Scout which united the rambling movement*

WHAT HAVE THE RAMBLERS EVER DONE FOR US?

The Ramblers' Association is the largest and most effective organisation representing walkers' interests.

TOP 10 PRIVATE LANDOWNERS: 1872

Title	Name of Landowner	Home County	Total acreage
Duke of	Sutherland	Sutherland	1,358,545
Duke of	Buccleuch & Queensbury	Northants	460,108
Earl of	Breadalbane	Perth	438,358
Lady	Matheson	Ross	424,560
Sir	Charles Ross Bt	Ross	356,500
Earl of	Seafield	Inverness	305,930
Duke of	Richmond and Gordon	Sussex	286,411
Earl of	Fife	Banff	249,220
Sir	Alexander Matheson Bt	Ross	220,663
Duke of	Atholl	Perth	201,640

TOP 10 PRIVATE LANDOWNERS: 2001

Title	Name of Landowner	Home County	Total acreage
Duke of	Buccleuch & Queensbury	Dumfries	270,900
Dukedom of	Atholl (Trustees)	Perth	148,000
Prince of	Wales	Cornwall	141,000
Duke of	Northumberland	Northumbs	132,200
Duke of	Westminster	Cheshire	129,300
Captain	A.A. Farquarson	Aberdeen	106,500
Earl of	Seafield	Banff	101,000
Viscount	Cowdray	Aberdeen	93,600
Mr	Robert Fleming	Argyll	88,900
Mr	Edmund Vesty	Sutherland	86,300

10 WALK-ON CAMEOS BY THE
MASTER OF SUSPENSE

Alfred Hitchcock made a brief appearance in each of his films. As there's nothing worse during the nail-biting final moments of a tense thriller than having someone shout out: 'Look, there he is. That's him in the grey suit at the back of the bus/the train/Mount Rushmore', he got most of his appearances out of the way in the earlier scenes. Here is a sample.

North By Northwest
Missing a bus ....Opening credits.
Frenzy
In crowd, wearing bowler hat...4 minutes in.
Psycho
Wearing cowboy hat, outside window. ....4 minutes in.
Marnie
In hotel corridor..5 minutes in.
To Catch A Thief
To Cary Grant's left on a bus...9 minutes in.
Vertigo
Walking down street...11 minutes in.
Dial M for Murder
In the reunion photo ....12 minutes in.
Topaz
Getting out of a wheelchair in airport..............................29 minutes in.
Spellbound
Coming out of a lift with a violin case..............................40 minutes in.
Suspicion
Posting a letter..47 minutes in.

HOLY WALKS

Bubastas was the centre for the cult of the Egyptian cat goddess Bastet from the 13th to 9th centuries BC. Situated 80km northeast of Cairo an estimated 700,000 pilgrims journeyed to the temple every year for an annual festival, which – according to some – celebrated with copious quantities of alcohol and free sex.

RAMBLING RIDDLE

One word follows the first word below and precedes the second to make two new words. What is it? Answer on page 153.
SILVER WALK

The Ramblers

ENJOY THE COUNTRYSIDE

How Paul laughed when he realised it was the same section of wall they'd passed five hours earlier.

QUOTE UNQUOTE

I will clamber through the clouds and exist
JOHN KEATS, poet

LONG WAY TO GO

Since 1900, Johann Hurlinger has held a record for walking. Over 55 days, he walked the 870 miles between Vienna and Paris. You may not think this is particularly exceptional... except for the fact that he completed the distance on his hands!

HOLY WALKS

Quetzalcoatl was an ancient god of civilisation and learning and a mix between a bird and a serpent. A temple dedicated to Quetzalcoatl was found north of Mexico City and discovered to be a site of pilgrimage – devotees visited this site from all over Mexico, and it is thought, elsewhere in South America.

WATER WALKS

LOWTIDE

LowTide is an international free festival that helps people explore inter-tidal sites under expert guidance. Discovery Walks take place along rivers and estuaries, while EcoFayres are larger events, combining inter-tidal walks with activities for children between the ages of seven and twelve, including interactive exhibitions and environmental games. LowTide is held annually on the Saturday in May with the lowest tide.

SEXUAL PLEASURES THAT WALKERS MIGHT ENJOY

Formicophilia, or entomophilia, is sexual arousal from having ants, or other insects, crawl over your body. Cleopatra is believed to have owned a box that, when filled with bees and placed against her genitals, provided her with the vibratory stimulation she was looking for when Mark Anthony wasn't in town.

QUOTE UNQUOTE

Walking, ideally, is a state in which the mind, the body, and the world are aligned, as though they were three characters finally in conversation together, three notes suddenly making a chord.
REBECCA SOLNIT,
writer on walking

A POTENTIAL RAMBLING ANTHEM...

...although it's already being used by someone else.

When you walk through a storm

The song is from the Rodgers and Hammerstein musical 'Carousel'. However, it is more well known as a hit for Gerry Marsden (Gerry and the Pacemakers), who had risen to fame with *Ferry 'cross the Mersey*.

The reason why the Kop at Liverpool FC adopted it is not really known. One story was that at the time that Gerry Marsden released the song, it was played at Anfield a few times before matches. Then one Saturday it wasn't played but the Kop started singing it anyway and it just grew from there, to the now traditional rendition before kick-off. Gerry Marsden sang the song at the last match of the Kop.

You'll never walk alone

QUOTE UNQUOTE

Climb the mountains and get their good tidings. Nature's peace will flow into you as sunshine flows into trees. The winds will blow their own freshness into you, and the storms their energy, while cares will drop off like autumn leaves.
JOHN MUIR, naturalist and writer

KEY WEBSITES TO CHECK BEFORE YOU GO

www.ramblers.org.uk
The one-stop shop for walkers. Information on every aspect of walking including footpath protection, freedom to roam, guided walks, accommodation, guidebooks and maps

www.ordnancesurvey.co.uk
Easy searching for walkers' maps

www.multimap.com or
www.streetmap.co.uk
Online mapping searchable by place name, postcode or OS grid reference

www.metoffice.com or
www.bbc.co.uk/weather
Detailed weather forecasts

www.nationalrail.co.uk
Journey planner on all National Rail services plus news on how services are running

www.traveline.org.uk
Journey planning and info for buses, trams, metro/underground, ferries (in Greater London use www.tfl.gov.uk – Transport for London)
(continued over)

www.visitbritain.com
Official tourism site which also includes a directory of tourist/visitor information centres in Britain – these are great sources of walking information

www.walkingwild.com
Information on walking in Scotland

www.nationaltrail.co.uk
Information about the National Trails of England and Wales

www.waterscape.com
Information on walking along waterways

www.whi.org.uk (Walking the way to Health Initiative)
For short, healthy walks near you

www.countryside.gov.uk
(Countryside Agency)
www.snh.org.uk
(Scottish Natural Heritage)
www.ccw.gov.uk
(Countryside Council for Wales)

www.yha.org.uk
www.syha.org.uk
Youth hostels in England/ Wales and Scotland respectively

http://countrywalks.defra.gov.uk
Paths and land open under 'agri-environment' schemes in England
See **www.ccw.gov.uk**
Land open under the similar 'Tir Gofal' scheme in Wales

www.englishnature.org.uk
National nature reserves in England (for NNRs in Scotland and Wales see SNH and CCW above)

www.forestry.gov.uk
(Forestry Commission) – open access woodland and forest parks throughout Britain

www.nationaltrust.org.uk
Large areas of protected historic countryside as well as built heritage, in England and Wales

www.nts.org.uk
(National Trust for Scotland) – as National Trust but for Scotland

www.rspb.org.uk
Open access bird and nature reserves throughout Britain

www.woodlandtrust.org.uk
Open access smaller, local woodlands throughout Britain

www.wildlifetrusts.org
Local nature reserves throughout Britain

www.era-ewv-ferp.org
(European Ramblers Association) – for information on European long distance footpaths and walking organisations
Tide tables

www.theaa.com/travelwatch/travel_news.jsp
Traffic news

And one key number to take with you:
Talking pages for taxis 0800 600 900

The sole criterion is to walk with the senses, with hands that feel, ears that hear, and eyes that see.
ROBERT BROWNE,
US writer

HOLY WALKS

Siwa Oasis in Egypt was the site for Ammon's oracle – the most powerful god of the ancient Egyptian empire. Worshipped also by Syrians, Libyans and Ethiopians, Alexander the Great – one of thousands who travelled there – was pronounced son of Ammon.

MAD FOR WALKING

Bill Irwin is an amazing man. This courageous Appalachian hiker was blinded by an eye disease at the age of 28. On March 8th 1990, Irwin, accompanied only by his dog, Orient, set out from Springer Mountain, Georgia during some of the worst floods in the state's history. Eight months later on November 21, Irwin arrived at Mount Katahdin, Maine, the first blind man to through-hike the Appalachian Trail. Despite breaking a rib, falling on countless occasions, and having many difficulties in persuading the well-trained Orient to guide him along such a dangerous path, his love of the mountains spurred him onwards.

QUOTE UNQUOTE

I nauseate walking; 'tis a country diversion, I hate the country.
WILLIAM CONGREVE, writer

THE EARLY DAYS

Early man is believed to have originated in the horn of Africa. But remains have been found very far from there – proving that our ancestors have walked a long way:

Name	Years Ago	Where Found
Dmanisi skull	1.75 million	Georgia
Java Man	700,000	Indonesia
Peking Man	420,000	China

BEAR FACTS

Polar bears can walk over enormous distances in the winter when the Arctic sea is frozen. One female polar bear who was fitted with a radio collar astounded scientists when she walked over an area of 30,000 square miles.

In Canada polar bears hunt seals in the spring, until the breaking ice forces them ashore – where there's nothing to eat. There they wander around until the ice reforms in a starving stupor – known locally as a 'walking hibernation'.

MASS HOMECOMING

In one day in December 1996 more than 450,000 people left their refugee camps in Tanzania and walked home to Rwanda.

QUOTE UNQUOTE

You have to stay in shape. My grandmother, she started walking five miles a day when she was 60. She's 97 today and we don't know where the hell she is.
ELLEN DEGENERES, comedian

9 THINGS TO AVOID STEPPING ON

Pink chewing gum
A puddle that slowly emerges from the corner of a dark alley
Your own pants • A sticky label
The little salady bits that fell out of someone's kebab last Friday
A splatter of diced carrots and peas
A banana skin smothered in butter on a patch of dry ice
Thin air

OH I DO LIKE TO BE BESIDE THE SEASIDE

In Victorian and Edwardian times visiting the seaside became a popular activity. However it was thought unladylike for the women to paddle in the sea, as this was undignified and something that only maids would do. The women would instead partake in an 'afternoon promenade'. Walking along the sea front became an essential part of the life of a resort with people coming to see and be seen.

SAS ADVICE ON HOW TO PREPARE
FOR A WALK IN BORNEO

You'll find the high spot of your day,' said the major, 'is cleaning your teeth. The only bit of you you can keep clean. Don't shave in the jungle, because the slightest nick turns septic at once. And don't take more than one change of clothes, because you must keep your Bergen weight well down below sixty pounds. And don't expect your Iban trackers to carry it for you, either, because they have enough to do transporting their own food. So keep one set of dry kit in a sealed bag in your pack. Get into that each night after you've eaten.

Powder yourself all over, too, with zinc talc – don't feel sissy about it – you'll halve the rashes and the rot and the skin fungus. Then sleep. Then get up at 5.30 and into your wet kit. It's uncomfortable at first, but don't weaken – ever; if you do, there'll be two sets of wet kit in no time, you'll lose sleep and lose strength and then there'll be a disaster. But take as many dry socks as you can. Stuff them into all the crannies in your pack. And, in the morning, soak the pairs you are going to wear in autan insect repellent, to keep the leeches out of your boots. Stick it on your arms and round your waist and neck and in your hair, too, while you're about it, but not on your forehead because the sweat carries it into your eyes and it stings. Cover yourself at night, too against the mosquitoes. Take them seriously, because malaria is a terrible thing and it's easy to get, pills or no.

Get some jungle boots, good thick trousers and strong shirts. You won't want to nancy about in shorts once the first leech has had a go at you, believe me. Acclimatise slowly. The tropics takes people in different ways. Fit young men here just collapse in Brunei. You'll think it's the end of the world. You can't breathe. You can't move.

And then after two weeks you'll be used to it. And once in the jungle proper you'll never want to come out.

Into the Heart of Borneo,
Redmond O'Hanlon

BOTTOM DWELLER

In 2003, Lloyd Scott from Rainham completed the first 'underwater marathon'. He spent 12 days walking 26 miles along the bottom of Loch Ness wearing a 1940s diving suit, complete with a 40lb metal helmet.

'Very lonely' was how he described the experience. And in case you're wondering: no, he didn't meet it.

RAMBLING RIDDLE

Charlotte decided to walk to the local wood, 10 miles away. As she set off, her dog ran from her side to the wood at a constant 8 mph. As soon as the dog reached the wood, it started the return journey to Charlotte, keeping to the same speed. The dog continued this behaviour until Charlotte reached the wood. If Charlotte kept to a constant 4 mph, how far did the dog run in total?

Answer on page 153.

WEATHER LORE FOR WALKERS

Red sky at night, shepherd's delight
Red sky in the morning, shepherd's warning.

This famous saying may well have originated abroad. In the Bible, Matthew xvi, 2, 3, Christ says:
'When it is evening, ye say, it will be fair weather: for the sky is red. And in the morning, it will be foul weather today: for the sky is red and lowering.'

There is truth in the saying. As any good shepherd could tell you, a pale rosy evening sky with little cloud is a sign of fair weather, haze particles causing the light to bend and creating the pinkish glow. About seven out of ten red sunsets herald good weather the following day. However, a deep red glow under thick cloud, often visible at sunset or at dawn, is a good indication of rain. The rich colour is caused by light bending through water droplets in the atmosphere.

7 NICE LONG TRAILS YOU MIGHT WANT TO TRY – BUT YOU WON'T BE ALONE

Thames Path National Trail: 527,000 visits during the summer months of 1999.

Ridgeway National Trail: 87,000 visits during the summer months of 1996.

Offa's Dyke Path National Trail: 120,000 people use this national trail each year.

Over 12,000 long-distance walkers and over 250,000 day ramblers use the **Pennine Way National Trail** every year.

Over 1 million visits are made to the **South West Coast Path National Trail** each year.

The Peddars Way and Norfolk Coast Path National Trail: 100,000 visits made per year.

50,000 people walk along some or all of the **West Highland Way** over the course of a year.

The first documented Land's End to John O'Groats (LEJOG) walk was in 1863 by an American called Elihu Burritt who walked from London to John O'Groats, and at a later date from London to Land's End. The first complete walk was by two brothers in 1871, John and Paul Naylor who set out on a wandering route with no maps and abstained from alcohol and tobacco as well as attending two religious services every Sunday.

Land's End and John O'Groats represent the two points furthest apart on the British mainland. Yet Dunnet's Head is in fact the most northerly position in Britain, whilst Lizard Point is the most southern.

The attempt to cover the whole distance from one point to another has become famously known around the world as the End to End.

Billy Butlin, the well known holiday camp entrepreneur gained the LEJOG its publicity. He organised the first ever challenge walk between the two points, offering prize money of over £5000.

In May 1990, Armind Pandya from India took 26 days, 7 hours to go End to End... backwards. He has similarly crossed the United States.

A 78-year-old man took just 40 days to complete the distance and proposed to his fiancée when he got there.

Two brothers-in-law took 30 days to push each other the length in a wheelbarrow.

A joiner from Newcastle walked the length with a wooden door on his back in 5 weeks.

The shortest possible LEJOG walk is currently 868 miles, 6 miles shorter than the signpost at Land's End states. (By avoiding traffic, you add an extra 6 miles).

Joe Lambert, a 9-year-old with diabetes, walked the entire length in 40 days in order to raise money for diabetic research.

WALKING WORDS

From binocular carriers to zimmer frame users, from twitchers to first-time birdwatchers, from entomologists to creepy-crawlyophobes, from budding botanists to lichenologists, you will find plenty of walks to enthrall, entertain and educate. Read all about 'em, then step back into real natural history.

David Bellamy's foreword to *Wildlife Walks*,
Think Publishing and The Wildlife Trusts

Weight, in pounds, of rocks dragged back from the South Pole by 35
Captain Scott

When walking it's important to think about your posture. Try leaning forward from your ankles instead of the waist. Leaning from the waist tires the back and makes breathing harder, try keeping your head level and your chin up.

Walk smoothly with long strides, putting energy into each step.

When walking up hills, poles or a long, lean stick can be useful. Although they will not change the amount of energy expended, poles shift some of the effort to your arms.

Allow your arms to swing naturally by your side to aid balance and conserve energy.

Walk from your heel to your toe, allowing you to 'push off' with your toes.

When walking along roads with no pavements, always walk facing the traffic except when you need to see round a right-hand bend. If it is dark remember to wear some reflective gear. It's easy for the walkers to see cars but not so easy for the cars to see you.

Walking is the safest form of aerobic exercise. It has the same benefits as such sports as running, swimming and rowing yet at a much lower injury risk rate. Even so, especially for older walkers, it is advisable to stretch your leg muscles, particularly the hamstrings and calves, before a long walk.

If walking alone, always tell someone where you're going, and when you plan to be back.

Take a mobile phone with you by all means but don't rely on it for getting you out of trouble, especially in hilly areas where reception is poor.

Just go out and have a walk!

QUOTE UNQUOTE

Walking is man's best medicine.
HIPPOCRATES, Ancient Greek physician

HOLY WALKS

Camina de Santiago is an 800km route from southern France across Northern Spain, to Santiago de Compostela. The site was originally founded by St James, whose body was also buried here after he was killed in Palestine. His remains were discovered in the 9th century and the area became a centre of pilgrimage for Christians, thousands of whom still walk there today.

In England and Wales you can walk along the following routes, so long as you stick to the line of the path:

• Public rights of way – the public have a legal right to use these: footpaths (for walking), bridleways (for walking, cycling and horse riding), byways (although these are legally open to all traffic and you may find motor bikes and off-road vehicles on them, they are used primarily by people on foot, horseback and pedal cycle) and restricted byways (open to walkers, cyclists, horse riders and non-motorised vehicles such as horse-drawn carts).

• Permissive paths – the landowner has given permission for the public to use them but may also withdraw that permission at any time.

• Multi-user routes such as cycle paths and 'greenways', and most towpaths (these are often suitable for wheelchairs, if you don't mind bicycles whizzing past).

• Most public roads, but take care.

• Named and signed 'promoted routes' such as National Trails (these are, for the most part, along public rights of way).

Most of these are shown on Ordnance Survey Explorer and Landranger maps.

You are also 'free to roam' across:

• Public parks and other open spaces managed for free public recreation.

• Most land owned by the National Trust, Foresty Commission and Woodland Trust as shown on Ordnance Survey Explorer maps.

• Land where access is by right or agreement as shown on OS Explorer maps, including most commons, and land on DEFRA's countryside walks register.

• Permissive access land, but permission may be withdrawn.

• Land with 'de facto' access such as most beaches and some areas of open country.

• Mountain, moor, heath, down and commons shown on official access maps produced by the Countryside Agency and Countryside Council for Wales, once new access rights are introduced.

In Scotland you can walk on nearly all paths, tracks and roads, rights of way, core paths and promoted routes, and across nearly all land provided you do so responsibly, except for the curtilage of buildings and land used for railways, airfields, harbours, defence and similar uses.

7 ODD SIGNS FOUND BY WALKERS

Height of this notice: 7 feet

Toilet. Stay in car

Hitchhikers may be escaping
inmates

Do not molest trees and shrubs

Private land owned by glue
factory. Please stick to path

Absolutely nothing for 27 miles

The farmer allows walkers to
cross the field for free, but the
bull charges

MADE FOR MOONWALKING

Armstrong's boots never came back to Earth. They were left behind in space before returning to Earth in case of contamination.

The shock-absorbing air spaces within a pair of Nike air trainers were originally developed for the boots of moonwalking astronauts. The composition of moonboots also includes an inner layer, connected to the Torso and Limb Suit Assembly (TLSA) consisting of 20-21 layered types of nylons and Kapton film surrounded by Teflon-coated glass fibre beta cloth. The outer layer, otherwise known as the Integrated Thermal Micrometeoroid Garment (ITMG), consists of metal-woven fabric or Chromel-R to resist high lunar surface temperatures.

The boots are covered by a silicon rubber sole.

Apollo 11 astronauts Neil Armstrong and Buzz Aldrin walked an area of 250 metres on the moon.

POTENTIAL RAMBLING ANTHEMS

The Cake Walk – Taj Mahal

**These Boots were made for
Walking**
Patsy Kline/Nancy Sinatra

Walking in the Air
from *The Snowman*

Ramblin' Blues
Robert Johnson

Walking on Sunshine
Katrina and the Waves.

Walking After Midnight
Loretta Lynn/Patsy Kline

Walking on the Moon
The Police

Walk this Way – Aerosmith

The Walk
Jimmy McCracklin

Ramblin' Man – Tom Paxton

Ramble On – Led Zeppelin

Alice Walker Writer and Pulitzer prize winner – best known for her book *The Color Purple*.

Joseph Walker American explorer from Missouri. Walker's Lake and Walker's Pass, both in Missouri, are named after him.

John Walker Chemist who invented the first friction matches.

John Walker Compiled the first rhyming dictionary published in 1775 – without a computer.

T-bone Walker One of America's best-loved blues musicians who revolutionised American music in the 1940s with his electric guitar.

Johnny Walker (aka Badruddin Quazi) Bollywood's most famous comedian, known as India's answer to Bob Hope.

John Walker Lindh The middle class kid from California who fought with the Taliban in Afghanistan and is now serving 20 years in jail in his home state.

Murray Walker Formula One commentator frequently 'very much mistaken'.

Jim Walker Wrote the National Trail Guide to the North Downs Way, with Neil Curtis.

William Walker The diver who saved parts of Winchester Cathedral from sinking by diving into the watery foundations and shoring them up with bags of cement.

Walker Miles Pseudonymic writer of field path rambles.

Johnny Walker The son of an Ayrshire farmer who created the famous blend known as Johnny Walker.

Henry Walker In the 1880s founded the company that now makes Walkers Crisps.

BY NAME, BY NATURE

In 1944 an HM Treasury survey found that Walker was the 12th most common name in England and Wales.

The name was originally an occupational alternative for a 'fuller', a person who cleansed and thickened cloth, often by using their feet. In medieval England 'fuller' was the preferred term in the South, while northerners opted for the more straightforward title 'walker'. The name is most common in cloth producing areas, such as Yorkshire. Early 'Walkers' include Richard le Walkere from Warwickshire (c1248) and Robert le Walker from York (1260).

HOW TO KEEP YOUR FOOD OUT OF REACH OF BEARS AND OTHER HUNGRY CRITTERS

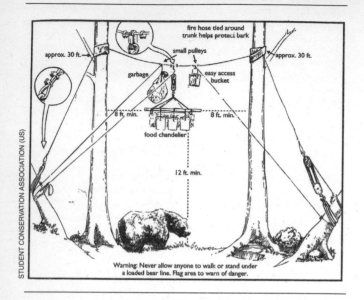

WALKING WORDS

Not until I went out could I tell that it was softly and coldly raining. Everything more than two or three fields away was hidden.

Cycling is inferior to walking in this weather, because in cycling chiefly ample views are to be seen, and the mist conceals them. You travel too quickly to notice many small things; you see nothing save the troops of elms on the verge of invisibility. But walking I saw every small thing one by one; not only the handsome gateway chestnut just fully dressed, and the pale green larch plantation where another chiff-chaff was singing, and the tall elm tipped by a linnet pausing and musing a few notes, but every primrose and celandine and dandelion on the banks, every silvered green leaf of honeysuckle up in the hedge, every patch of brightest moss, every luminous drop on a thorn tip. The world seemed a small place: as I went between a row of elms and a row of beeches occupied by rooks, I had a feeling that the road, that the world itself, was private, all theirs; and the state of the road under their nests confirmed me. I was going hither and thither to-day in the neighbourhood of my stopping place, instead of continuing my journey.

In Pursuit of Spring, Edward Thomas

HOW TO PACK A RUCKSACK

Heavy items should be packed close to your centre of gravity to make carrying your rucksack more comfortable. Pack heavy items close to your back and high in the rucksack, making the weight even across the width to prevent lean.

Pack lightly, but pack well. Only take essential items.

Always take too much water. You can never have enough. When it starts to weigh you down, start drinking. On strenuous climbs, start off with about 3 litres in your pack.

Don't take canned food. With the wide range of dehydrated food available in the UK, there is no need to take bulky cans on your long-distance walks. Cans are also sharp when opened, and if disposed of in litter collection areas, even in national parks, they are unlikely to be recycled.

Pack by meal. For example, if you are taking rice, measure it out beforehand and pack it with the accompanying ingredients in a single freezer bag.

Use different coloured bags to store individual items for easy indentification.

Roll clothing tightly and stuff it in waterproof bags or nylon 'stuff sacks' that are available from camping supply shops. Surround hard and angular items with clothing to stop them jabbing your back.

Pack your first aid in your rucksack, but keep plasters and minor first aid in your pockets.

QUOTE UNQUOTE

I have two doctors, my left leg and my right.
GEORGE M TREVELYAN, historian

WALK LIKE AN ANIMAL

Believe it or not, some snake species possess legs. Although there is no scientific evidence that the vestigial limbs found on the Cape Dwarf Burrowing Skink, and Large-scaled grass lizard are used for walking, there is further fossil evidence that snakes used to walk. The discovery of a fossil snake with legs was made in a limestone quarry north of Jerusalem. The fossil snake, which lived 95 million years ago, is named *Haasiophis terrasanctus*. It is a little over a metre long and has hind legs about 2cm long that extend all the way to the toe bones. Some scientists believe Pachyrachis represents the most primitive snake known and provides evidence of a link between mosasaurs: giant swimming lizards of the Cretaceous Period – and true snakes.

Graceland

Elvis Presley's home and refuge from the world, Graceland, welcomes over 600,000 visitors each year. Attendance ranges from a few hundred visitors on a weekday in the dead of winter to over 4,000 daily in July at the height of the travel season.

The total economic impact on the city of Memphis from Graceland visitors is estimated at over $150 million per year. And the city also greatly benefits from the intense worldwide publicity that Graceland and the Elvis Presley phenomenon continually bring to Memphis. Graceland employs 350 people on an annual basis, a number that can swell to as many as 450 in a busy summer season. Over half of Graceland's visitors are under the age of 35.

FOOT PHRASES THAT AREN'T ABOUT FEET

Foot the bill –
pay for a meal

My Foot! –
I don't believe it

Don't put a foot wrong –
make no mistakes

Put one's foot down –
either to insist that something is done, or to speed up in a car

Put your foot in it –
commit a blunder or indiscretion

Set on foot –
get things started

Have a foot in both camps –
to support both sides

Wrong-foot someone –
put someone at a disadvantage

Start on the wrong foot –
to make a mistake at the very beginning

On friendly-footing –
a good relationship

Firm-footing –
a solid foundation

Light footed –
to be nimble

Footloose and fancy free –
free from romantic ties

Follow in someone's footsteps –
to do the same as someone else

To tread underfoot –
to beat all the opposition

Footnote –
comment at bottom of page

GHOSTLY FOOTSTEPS

The ghost of a white lady has apparently been appearing for hundreds of years walking on what used to be known as the Great North Road near Aycliffe. She is said to have been picked up several times by stage coaches on the A167, but she has also made some more recent appearances. In 1978 motorist Dennis Fisher saw a woman in a white pixie hat and raincoat who floated across the road in a circle of blue light at 2am as he was heading for a night shift in the local colliery. The lady apparently had no face or legs.

THE STILE COUNSEL

The Ladder Style Stile
A ladder stile is put up after a stone or brick wall has been constructed and resembles a household ladder. They are usually used to prevent damage to the wall.

The Falling Style Stile
This clever invention resembles a fence but is actually a movable stile. If you push on one end the poles fall downwards enabling you to step, not leap, climb and stumble over. The weights on the opposite end cause the poles to bounce back into place when released.

The Step Style Stile
This can either be one raised platform embedded perpendicular to a wall or a set of raised stepping blocks, resembling a staircase, mounting a wall.

The Squeezer Style Stile
This type of clambering approach is narrow and tapers at the bottom to prevent livestock from passing through. It is usually constructed to allow a pedestrian of normal build to pass through sideways.

This type of stile is often found on top of step stiles.

NOT QUITE LIKE JESUS

An annual Walking on Water competition takes place at the University of San Diego. It is held to promote fundamental design, engineering and scientific principles and participants have reached speeds of about 50 metres per minute. The world record for walking on water is held by Remy Bricka who strolled across the Atlantic Ocean, leaving from Tenerife and arriving in Trinidad 40 days later. Remy also holds the record for the fastest walk across water covering a kilometre of an Olympic size swimming pool in 7 minutes 7 seconds.

His secret? Detachable polystyrene skis attached to the feet.

Julie and Gavin were having such an enjoyable time that they failed to notice four alien Marge Simpsons loom behind them

---

QUOTE UNQUOTE

In every walk with Nature one receives far more than he seeks.
JOHN MUIR, naturalist and writer

Reflexology

Reflexology is a natural healing art based on the principle that there are reflexes in the hands, feet and ears corresponding to every part, gland and organ of the body. Through application of pressure on these reflexes, reflexology can relieve tension, improve circulation and promote the natural function of the body.

In the pre-footwear past, human beings stimulated their reflexes naturally by walking barefoot over rocks, stones and rough ground but in the modern world we have lost touch with much of nature's way of maintaining equilibrium. Reflexology helps to restore this balance and promote natural health and vitality.

Reflexology has been practised for thousands of years in India, China and Egypt. An ancient Egyptian wall painting of the 6th Dynasty (circa 2400 BC) found in the tomb of Ankhmahor, an ancient Egyptian physician, depicts two men working on the feet and hands of two other men. Reflexology has also been used as a healing therapy by native Americans for generations, and is thought to have been passed down by the Inca civilisation.

Although reflexology does not diagnose or treat specific ailments, it has proved highly successful over time in relieving symptoms and easing pain or discomfort in the body, mentally and physically, as a result of stress, trauma or disease.

Reflexology is growing more popular primarily because we experience high levels of stress in our lives, which aggravates symptoms of other diseases or conditions. Reflexology is a very effective treatment for reducing stress.

Perhaps another reason for reflexology's increasing popularity is that although many people try to eat organic and fresh food some of these 'healthy' foods are grown in soil conditions with fewer basic minerals and nutrients than in the days of our grandparents. The lack of minerals puts a lot of pressure on our immune system, but reflexology assists the body in healing itself and normalising functions.

People are beginning to accept alternative remedies and natural health care, as these tend to focus on maintenance of the body with the aim of all-round well-being. Reflexology offers an all-natural therapy that does not require anything other than gentle manipulation to stimulate the body's natural healing mechanisms to regulate and heal. It is becoming one of the most popular methods of natural therapy, and the word is spreading further.

Information taken with thanks from www.aboutreflexology.com.

RAMBLING RIDDLE

One word follows the first word below and precedes the second to
make two new words or phrases. What is it?
CRESCENT WALK
Answer on page 153.

10 HEEL PHRASES THAT
AREN'T ABOUT HEELS

Come to heel
to obey or submit

Follow on the heels of
to follow close behind

Well-heeled
well paid, well armed

Show a clean pair of heels
to make a sharp exit

Down at heel
shabbily dressed

Turn on one's heel
turn round abruptly

Kick up one's heels
have a lively time

Cool one's heels
to wait a long time

Lay by the heel
to arrest and subdue someone

Dig one's heels in
to be stubborn or resist a request

HOT FOOTING IT

Fire walking has been practised by people throughout the world for
more than 3,000 years. In Japan thousands of people walk through
fires in rituals every spring. How do they not burn their feet? According
to an American professor of Physics who also holds the world record
for fire-walking, the answer lies in conductivity. Some materials – like
metal and sand – conduct heat more efficiently than others. Wood does
not conduct heat very well, enabling people to walk across burning
wood without serious injury.

WATER WALKS

AMROTH TO SAUNDERSFOOT AND TENBY, PEMBROKESHIRE
Amroth is on the South Pembrokeshire coast, at the start of the 186-
mile Pembrokeshire Coastal Path. The route to Tenby is around seven
miles long and takes 2.5 hours to walk, following the eastern portion
of the Pembrokeshire Coastal Path. Although the coastal path
generally follows the coast, at low tide it is possible to walk on the
sands between Amroth and Saundersfoot.

Don Betty has been walking across suspension bridges for 25 years, his unusual pastime having taken him to bridges all over the world. In 1995, he was entered into the Guinness Book of World Records as the person who has walked across more suspension bridges than anyone else in the world. Betty's obsession began in 1971, when he traversed a rope swing bridge suspended 240 feet across a canyon in British Columbia. Since then, he has crossed 22 of the 25 longest bridges in North America and 22 of the top 25 in the world. Betty has walked across the Golden Gate Bridge in San Francisco five times, and in 1989, he witnessed a suicide on the famous landmark. He has no plans to give up his hobby, despite recently having had an artificial leg fitted and undergoing open heart surgery – these hindrances have merely made taking photos of bridges more difficult. Betty's future plans include tackling bridges in Japan, Hong Kong, Denmark, Sweden and France.

QUOTE UNQUOTE

It is good to collect things; it is better to take walks.
ANATOLE FRANCE, French writer

EROTIC FEET

In 1992 the Duchess of York was photographed having her toe sucked by her financial adviser John Bryan. She was still married to Prince Andrew at the time.

10 TOE PHRASES THAT AREN'T ABOUT TOES

On one's toes – alert, eager

Toeing the line – conforming

A toe-hold – a small foothold

Turn up one's toes – to die

Walk on tiptoe – walk quietly

Toey – restless

Toe in the water – a test

Tread on someone's toes – to offend someone with a tactless remark

Keep someone on his toes – keep someone alert and attentive

Toerag – a person you don't respect

A MANSA FOR ALL SEASONS

Mansa Musa has gone down in history because of his amazing pilgrimage completed between 1324 and 1325. He was a wealthy king from Mali who followed the Islamic faith, as many others did after it had spread across Africa between 700 and 800 AD. In 1324, he undertook the required hajj or pilgrimage to Mecca. However, he made sure he did it in style. He is said to have taken more than 500 slaves with him and each one carried a staff of solid gold. He also took thousands of his subjects as well as his senior wife and her 500 attendants. When he passed through Cairo, Mansa Musa gave away so much gold that the price of gold fell and the economy was affected for 12 years.

The pilgrimage made a deep impression and Mali began to appear on maps throughout the Middle East and Europe, and sub-Saharan Africa was well known north of the Sahara for the first time.

Mansa Musa also brought back with him an Arabic library, religious scholars and the Muslim architect al-Sahili, who built the great mosques at Gao and Timbuktu and a royal palace.

SEXUAL PLEASURES THAT WALKERS MIGHT ENJOY

Psychrotentiginosity is the sexual arousal from being cold, or watching others who are cold. Magnus Hirschfeld, in his book Sexual Anomalies and Perversions, wrote that 'the thought and sight of chilly dress or pictorial representations of it, induce in me considerable erotic pleasure.'

POTENTIAL RAMBLING ANTHEMS

Walter's Walk – Led Zeppelin

Walk Away – Christina Aguilera

A walk – Bad Religion

I walk the earth my darling
Voice of the Beehive

Take a walk on the wild side
Lou Reed

Walking Backwards for Christmas – The Goons

Walk of Life – Dire Straits

(I saw you and him) Walking in the Rain —Oran Juice Jones

Walk Tall – Cannonball Adderley

Walking in Rhythm – The Blackbyrds

Walking Down Lonely Street – Joe Simon

Keep on Walking – Roy Ayers

Age of the oldest Olympic medallist, (who competed in the 50K walk in 1948)

Bealach

A shortish pass, generally one that crosses a low point between two hills.

Brocken spectre

This is an extraordinary optical sight that is usually experienced in hilly areas, particularly when you are close to cloud level, or standing in misty conditions. When the sunlight is strong and behind you, you will be able to see a huge shadow of yourself on the cloud wall. On a good day, the shadow will be ringed with a halo.

Col

This is the low point on a ridge between two peaks.

Coire

A Gaelic term for a hollow, usually backed by a ridge or plateau and often containing a small lochan. Coires are found in glaciated mountains.

Cornice

An overhanging wall of snow formed by the wind and found at the tops of gullies and steep slopes. Beware: it can easily break away.

SAY CHEESE

The foot has more sweat glands per square centimetre than any other part of the body – 250,000 sweat glands for each foot.

Each foot produces about a cup of sweat every day, and this combined with bacteria produces gases similar to those produced by bacteria in making cheese. Because we wear shoes, sweat cannot evaporate and the warm moisture surrounding the foot encourages the fungal infection known as athlete's foot.

Hyperhydrosis is when the sweat glands in the foot become over active and produce excessive amounts of perspiration. Most common in adolescents and young adults, how much we

sweat is mainly controlled by our metabolism but it can also be affected by anxiety, stress, and excessive fluids.

Bromhydrosis occurs when the bacterium which actually helps to decompose perspiration remains in shoes, leaving behind a foul smell. People who suffer from Anhydrosis have the opposite problem – a lack of perspiration.

Pitted Keratolysis is an infection caused by a bacterium which often occurs in soldiers who wear boots in humid conditions. If you notice a pitted honeycomb appearance on the skin of your feet, and they're beginning to smell truly atrocious, seek help from a doctor.

William Davies

Born in 1627, Davies was a farmer who supplemented his wages robbing the wealthy on Bagshot Heath and Salisbury Plain. Adept at disguising himself, he even robbed his own landlord, relieving him of the year's rent he had just paid. Unlike his contemporaries, who tended to have short careers, Davies continued moonlighting as a highwayman for 40 years, until he was shot during a coach holdup in 1690.

Katherine Ferrers

Born in 1662, the wife of a Lord in Hemel Hempstead, Katherine Ferrers supposedly took to the roads out of boredom with Ralph Chandler, a local farmer. Wounded during a holdup in 1684, she died at home and subsequently became known as the Wicked Lady Ferrers.

Moll Cutpurse

Born in 1589, tomboy Mary Frith was trained to make clothes but became far more adept at picking gentlemen's purses out of them – apparently her long fingers helped. Known for dressing as a man, she swaggered around the streets of London with a sword, and ran a gang of thieves who robbed coaches in Hounslow Heath. After relieving a prominent Republican of his money, she was sent to Newgate prison, but managed to bribe her way out. After this Mary decided to retire – and sell stolen goods instead! She was a resourceful woman – after being arrested for wearing gentlemen's clothes, she arranged for all her friends to pickpocket the crowd who turned up at her sentencing – who died naturally in 1659.

John Rann

Initially a coachman with a taste for fashionable clothes, John Rann was born in 1750. Known as '16 String Jack' – for the number of ribbons he wore round his breeches. John was a busy highwayman, who stopped coaches in Epping Forest and was tried and acquitted six times for robbery before eventually being caught with a victim's watch and hanged in 1774.

MODERN PILGRIMAGES

The Kumbh Mela is a festival that occurs every 12 years in Allahabad, India. Millions of people come to bathe in the sacred waters of the Ganges where it is believed all sins are purified. Up to as many as 45 million people visit.

Although often considered primarily a Hindu pilgrimage, the Kumbh Mela is a celebration of spiritual and planetary consequences that affect all humankind.

22 SOAP CHARACTERS WHO SHOULDN'T HAVE GONE OUT WALKING THAT DAY

Life can be very dangerous in soaps. Characters are up to seven times more likely to die while out walking than the general population, and of them all, the most dangerous place to be is Albert Square. EastEnders characters are more likely to die than Formula One drivers, bomb disposal experts and steeplejacks! Here's a sample of the accidents that have befallen soap characters while taking a stroll:

EastEnders

1990	Den Watts	Shot while walking along the canal
1990	Eddie Royle	Shot while out walking Roly
1995	Debbie Bates	Killed in a hit-and-run accident
1999	Tiffany Mitchell	Knocked down by Frank Butcher
2002	Jamie Mitchell	Knocked down by Martin Fowler

Coronation Street

1961	Ida Barlow	Knocked down by a bus
1964	Susan Schofield	Knocked down by a car
1986	Pat Bradley	Knocked down by a car
1989	Brian Tilsley	Stabbed outside a night club
1989	Alan Bradley	Knocked down by a tram in Blackpool
1993	Lisa Duckworth	Knocked down by a car
1997	Joyce Smedley	Knocked down by a car
2000	Alison Webster	Ran in front of a lorry

Brookside

1987	Lucky the dog	Squashed by a car
1987	Damon Grant	Stabbed to death in York
1998	Marcus Seddon	Fell off a cliff
2000	Susanna Farnham	Fell downstairs on the way to her wedding
2002	Rob Dexter	Threw himself in front of a van
2002	Imelda Clough	Drowned in a pond in the woods

Neighbours

1991	Kerry Bishop	Shot while protesting at a duck shoot
1992	Harold Bishop	Washed out to sea on a camping trip but returned 5 years later
1993	Todd	Hit by a van

5 HILL WALKING TERMS YOU'VE ALWAYS JUST PRETENDED TO KNOW

Donalds

Hills over 2,000 feet high in the Scottish Lowlands. Yet not all hills above this height are Donalds. There is a grading system the higher you go.

The next stage up finds the Grahams which stand at 2,000–2,499ft high; these are followed by the Corbetts that span 2,500–3,000ft, and then the Munros, that stand at over 3,000ft.

Gabbro

Rough, crystalline igneous rock forming much of the Cuillin Ridge in Skye. Tends to be black or dark brown.

Glissade

To slide down a snow slope using boots for skis. This is a good trick to pull off if you can do it, but highly embarrassing and even more highly dangerous if you can't.

Howff

A shelter found in the mountains. This is often a structure based around a boulder that has been bolstered against the weather with rocks and plant material. Useful in an emergency, or for the adventurous, but considerably less comfortable than a good tent.

Lapse Rate

The difference in temperature experienced by a climber between the base of a hill or mountain and the summit. In parts of Scotland, the lapse rate can be as much as 10°C.

Roughly speaking, an isotherm map for a hill based on annual mean temperatures would have contours showing a 1.7°C to 2.8°C drop in temperature for every 300 metres gained. So a Munro (see Donalds) might be some 6° or 7°C colder – and that does not take into account the effect of wind-chill.

RAMBLING RIDDLE

One word follows the first word below and precedes the second to make two new words or phrases. What is it?

JAY ABOUT

Answer on page 153.

EROTIC FEET

Feet can be a source of sexual gratification – both painful and pleasurable. This can involve the pain of having a stiletto heel ground into a sensitive part of the body or the pleasure of having the foot cleaned with a tongue. Crumbling food between the toes reportedly adds to this pleasure!

WEATHER LORE FOR WALKERS

If the moon rises haloed round;
Soon you'll tread on deluged ground

A blurred or watery moon or a solar halo is caused by the ice crystals in altostratus or cirrostratus clouds – the clouds are a sure sign of a rainbelt approaching, probably within five to eight hours

WALKING WORDS

How much you get from walking will depend, in the last resort, upon yourself, rather than the country. One mind will get more out of a few fields than another will from a range of mountains. It is a matter of developing a breadth of interests.

For myself, I love all historical things, and , though knowing not the first elements of architecture, derive pleasure from castles, cathedrals, inns and cottages. For the minutiae of Nature I have no aptitude. I am continually and infuriatingly baffled by my inability to name the little hedges, the birds, and other retiring beauties of the country.

The ideal walker would, I suppose, have geology and all other –olo-gies at his fingertips. He would be steeped in history and literary asso-ciations. He would be able to analyse a cathedral into its constituent parts and tag each with a date and style. He would talk knowledgeably to the locals about crops and crafts and industries. Such a man (supposing his head did not burst) would cover about one mile in a summer's day. I prefer to air my ignorance on the hills and walk twen-ty, noticing what I can. But certainly a little knowledge of all or any of these things, far from being dangerous, adds immensely to one's pleasure.

Walking in England, Geoffrey Trease

SPICE UP YOUR LIFE

The spices in your cupboard can tickle your tastebuds but they can also be used to warm up cold feet. Just combine 1 tablespoon of cayenne powder and 1 teaspoon of ginger powder – mix together and sprinkle 1/8 teaspoon into a pair of socks – and slide your chilled piggies inside. The combination of muscle-warming cayenne and muscle-relaxing gin-ger works wonders to ease tired feet, whether you're kicking back and relaxing, sleeping or walking around. It is a gradual warming but lasts for a few hours. This powder combo does stain so use dark socks or socks that are expendable. Also, if you have any cuts, this powder can really sting. Keep away from your eyes also, and wash your hands thor-oughly after touching the mixture.

10 DIRECTORS WITH WALK-ON PARTS IN THEIR OWN FILMS

Taxi Driver	Director Martin Scorsese was the sick man who gets into Robert De Niro's taxi and claims his wife is having an affair.
Apocalypse Now	Director Francis Ford Coppola appeared as a TV director who is filming the war in the background.
Tootsie	Director Sidney Pollack was Dustin Hoffman's agent.
Chinatown	Director Roman Polanski appeared on the street with a flick knife and slit Jack Nicholson's nose. Jack was forced to wear a bandage for the rest of the film.
The Treasure of Sierra Madre	Director John Huston played a wealthy man who continually gave Humphrey Bogart handouts.
Platoon	Director Oliver Stone played an army general whose bunker was blown up by a North Vietnamese suicide bomber.
The Blues Brothers	Director John Landis appeared as a state trooper.
Indiana Jones and the Temple of Doom	Director Stephen Spielberg appeared as a tourist at the airport.
Spinal Tap	Rob Reiner appeared as the group's documentary film maker.
The Matrix	The Wachowski brothers appeared as window cleaners.

QUOTE UNQUOTE

Before supper walk a little; after supper do the same.
DESIDERIUS ERASMUS ROTERODAMUS,
Dutch humanist and theologian

Ian, his finger superglued to the map, tried to call to passers by for help, when he realised his pipe was superglued to his lips, too

BE A CENTURION

A Centurion is someone who has walked or run 100 miles in 24 hours.

The Long Distance Walkers' Association organises a 100-mile Challenge every year over the spring bank holiday. If you'd like to join in, see www.ldwa.org.uk.

Meanwhile, the Olympic race-walk long distance is 50K, which equals 31 miles and takes top walkers 3 hrs 40 mins. Imagine walking at a speed of seven minutes per mile over that distance.

Borley rectory in Essex has been branded the most haunted building in England. It was built on the site of an old monastery where according to legend, a monk was caught eloping with a nun, who was bricked up alive in the nunnery eight miles away. Hauntings apparently started in 1885 with the sighting of a sad little nun. A year later a servant resigned in fear of ghostly footprints.

The sightings have worsened over the years, culminating in bells ringing, writing appearing on walls, lights being turned on and stones being thrown from nowhere. The rectory was burnt down in an accident in 1939.

WALKING WITH POLES

A person who is 5'6" and weighs 155-165 pounds and walks with a stride length of 70-80% of their height (4.76 feet or 2.3 feet per step) at a 3 mph pace will experience about 192 pounds of peak force per foot strike. Over the course of a mile, this accumulates to 425,856 pounds of peak force transmitted to the lower extremity. Research has shown that by walking with poles an individual can reduce the force per foot strike by about 2-4% (5.76 pounds of peak force). Thus, over the course of that same mile, the lower extremity is spared approximately 6 tons of peak force.

THE GOOD FOOT DOCTOR

William Scholl was born in 1882 and even as a teenager he exhibited a fascination with shoes and footcare. He started out as his family's cobbler, being one of 13 children. He then moved to Chicago as an apprentice to a shoemaker, attended medical school at night and received his medical degree in 1904 at the age of 22. Scholl then went on to patent his first foot supporting shoe. He gradually assembled a staff of consultants who travelled the country giving lectures on proper foot maintenance. He also published books to widen knowledge on footcare, including the Dictionary of the Foot (1916).

Scholl helped launch the 'Cinderella Foot Contest' in 1916 to find the most perfect female feet. A Cinderella was chosen after tens of thousands of entries and the careful scrutiny of their feet.

The pictures of the 'perfect feet' inspired, as had been hoped, thousands of Americans to compare their own feet to the perfect feet and, as they inevitably found discrepancies, to rush out and buy his footcare products.

William Scholl died in 1968, aged 86. He always said that while others never forgot a face, he never forgot a foot.

HOLY WALKS

Asclepius was a Greek hero who became god of medicine. A sanctuary was set up in his name in Epidaurus in the Peloponnese where invalids came to be cured in their thousands in the 3rd century BC.

QUOTE UNQUOTE

Why, one day in the country
Is worth a month in the town
CHRISTINA ROSSETTI, writer

WALKING WORDS

Now, to be properly enjoyed, a walking tour should be gone upon alone. If you go in company, or even in pairs, it is no longer a walking tour in anything but name; it is something else and more in the nature of a picnic. A walking tour should be gone upon alone, because freedom is of the essence; because you should be able to stop and go on, and follow this way or that, as the freak takes you; and because you must have your own pace, and neither trot alongside a champion walker, nor mince in time with a girl.

Walking Tours,
Robert Louis Stevenson

HOW TO MOONWALK

You too can walk like Michael Jackson.
Just follow these simple steps.

Stand with your right foot slightly ahead of your left and bend the right knee and place your weight on your right toes.

Now switch the weight to your left toes and bend your left knee.

Keeping the pressure on your left toes, slide your right foot back, using the heel, not the toes.

Drop the right heel when it passes the left foot, but keep on sliding until the right foot is comfortably behind you while still flat.

Bend your right knee so the weight shifts to the right toes. Slide that left foot back, dropping your heel as it passes the right foot.

Keep on pushing the left leg back until it's behind you.

Repeat until bored.

WALKING BUSES

From Aberdeen to Eastbourne, from Cardiff to Clacton-on-Sea, walking buses are being trialled by schoolchildren and their parents. A 'Walking Bus' allows a group, or 'bus', of children to walk safely to school every day, supervised by trained adult guides. This is an alternative to the school run, and is an effective means by which to achieve the government's targets of reducing traffic and providing safe pedestrian routes.

The scheme can also benefit children's health, since walking helps children's hearts, aids in building up their muscles, strengthens their bones, makes them more alert and sociable and improves their academic performance. Walking buses also teach kids road safety, a vital skill for their later lives. The other aim of the scheme is to reduce traffic congestion in the mornings, since twenty per cent of traffic between 8 and 9am is on the school run. If you'd like to find out more information visit **www.walkingbus.org.**

ROLY SMITH'S 10 CLASSIC BACKPACKING TRAILS

Roly Smith writes about the great outdoors.

The Appalachian Trail – 3,379km from Maine to Georgia, USA

Pennine Way – 434km from Edale to Kirk Yetholm, Great Britain

The Pacific Crest Trail – 4,119km from Mexico to the Canadian Border

The South West Coast Path – 829km from Minehead to Poole, England

The Milford Track – 53km from Lake Te Anau to Milford Sound, New Zealand

The West Highland Way – 150km from Glasgow to Fort William, Scotland

The E1 – 2,767km from the North Sea to the Mediterranean, across Europe

The Dingle Way – 183km around the Dingle Peninsula, Ireland

The Tour du Mont Blanc – 116km around Europe's highest peak

The Ulster Way – 917km around the six counties of Northern Ireland

6 SOAP PETS WHO REALLY SHOULDN'T HAVE GONE WALKIES THAT DAY

Characters fare badly in soaps, but animals are the least fortunate of them all! Some animals do better than others: a dog's destiny in Brookside Close is to be run over, but in Neighbours, it is to survive beyond all possible odds.

Coronation Street
1997   Theresa the Turkey ....Knocked over by Les Battersby's car
EastEnders
1993   Roly...Hit by a car
Brookside
1987   Lucky ....Squashed by a car
1997   Cracker ....Reversed over by a van
2000   Minty .... Driven over by Ray
Neighbours
1989   Bouncer ....Knocked over by Paul Robinson
1991   Bouncer ....Knocked over by Dorothy Burke
1991   Bouncer ....Trapped in a hole in the quarry
1993   Bouncer ....Kidnapped

A MAN WALKS INTO A BAR...

... with a roll of tarmac under his arm and says:
'Pint please, and one for the road'.

WALKING WORDS

Who is the third who walks always beside you?
When I count, there are only you and I together
But when I look ahead up the white road
There is always another one walking beside you
Gliding wrapt in a brown mantle, hooded
I do not know whether a man or a woman
– But who is that on the other side of you?
The Wasteland, TS Eliot

In a footnote to these lines, Eliot wrote that they were 'stimulated by the account of one of the Antarctic expeditions (I forget which, but I think one of Shackleton's): it was related that the party of explorers, at the extremity of their strength, had the constant delusion that there was one more member than could actually be counted.'

FOOT NOTES

The feet contain a quarter of all the bones in the body.

Each foot has a network of more than 100 tendons, muscles and ligaments.

Feet have 250,000 sweat glands. When active, feet can produce four to six ounces of perspiration a day, sometimes more.

Women have about four times as many foot problems as men. High heels are one of the main reasons for this.

Your feet mirror your general health. Conditions such as arthritis, diabetes, nerve and circulatory disorders can show their initial symptoms in the feet – so check any foot ailments carefully as they can be your first sign of more serious medical problems.

Walking barefoot can cause plantar warts. The virus enters through a cut.

About 5% of the population have toenail problems in a given year.

RAMBLING RIDDLE

Unravel the following:
gniklaw happinesshappiness
Answer on page 153.

QUOTE UNQUOTE

I had better admit right away that walking can in the end become an addiction… even in this final stage it remains a delectable madness, very good for sanity, and I recommend it with passion.
COLIN FLETCHER, writer

HOLY WALKS

Mount Kailash is a pilgrimage site in Tibet revered by Hindus, Buddhist, Jains and Bonpos. A single circuit of the 32km route round the base will – according to some – ease the sins of a lifetime. The pilgrimage continued for thousands of years until the Chinese invasion of Tibet. Now only 200 pilgrims are allowed to enter the site from India. To join them you would have to enter a lucky draw run by the Indian government, and undergo two days of physical tests in a Delhi hospital to make sure you are fit enough. After all, the site is 22,028 feet high.

National Parks

National Parks hold the greatest protection of landscape of any designation in Great Britain. They are special areas created to conserve and enhance their natural beauty, wildlife and cultural heritage, and promote enjoyment and understanding of them by the public. There are 13 parks in total, across England, Wales and Scotland, with two new parks (the New Forest and the South Downs) currently in the process of being designated.

Areas of Outstanding Natural Beauty (AONBs)

AONBs are designated areas in England and Wales and are protected and managed by the local authorities whose territory includes part of their area. They are, by law, equal to national parks in landscape value.

National Scenic Areas (NSAs)

These are the Scottish equivalents of AONBs. They are sites considered to be of national significance on the basis of their outstanding scenic interest or unsurpassed attractiveness which must be conserved as part of the country's natural heritage.

Sites of Special Scientific Interest (SSSIs)

SSSIs are sites which are particularly important for their wildlife and geology, much of which would be irreplaceable if they were lost from our landscape.

National Nature Reserves (NNRs)

Nationally recognised priority areas for wildlife. Many are also designated as SSSIs. Many are open to the public.

Local Nature Reserves (LNRs)

For protecting wildlife and geological features locally.

Natural Areas

These provide a way of interpreting the ecological variations of the country in terms of natural features, illustrating the distinctions between one area and another.

Country Parks

Enhance the opportunities for recreation and exercise, especially for city dwellers.

Community Forests

Enhance the relatively low level of tree coverage in the UK.

Heritage Coasts

In England and Wales only.

International designations

• RAMSAR sites are set up to protect wetlands.
• Special Protection Areas (SPAs) are set aside for birds.
• Special Areas of Conservation (SACs) protect natural habitats both at sea and on land.
• World Heritage Sites are internationally recognised sites of either natural or cultural significance such as Stonehenge or Hadrian's Wall.

As Gordon watched his son walk like an Egyptian yet again, he couldn't help wondering if there was something Jenny hadn't told him.

---

20 REASONS TO STAY AT HOME

Don't walk in Britain if you suffer from:

Acarophobia ....fear of mites or ticks
Acrophobia ....fear of being in high places
Agoraphobia ....fear of open spaces
Ambulophobia ....fear of walking
Anemophobia ....fear of wind
Apiphobia ....fear of bees
Bathmophobia ....fear of steep slopes
Batrachophobia..fear of frogs
Brontophobia ....fear of thunder
Catapedaphobia ....fear of jumping from high and low places
Cryophobia....................................fear of frost, ice or extreme cold
Eleutherophobia..fear of freedom
Gephyrophobia ....fear of bridges or of crossing them
Hylophobia ....fear of forests
Karaunophobia ....fear of lightning
Limnophobia ....fear of lakes
Myrmecophobia ....fear of ants
Ombrophobia..fear of rain
Potamophobia ....fear of rivers
Taurophobia..fear of bulls

---

62 *Year, in the 18th century, in which the Earl of Sandwich first ate a piece of salt beef between two slices of toast*

I spent the... day roaming through the valley. I stood beside the sources of the Arveiron, which take their rise in a glacier, that with slow pace is advancing down from the summit of the hills, to barricade the valley. The abrupt sides of vast mountains were before me; the icy wall of the glacier overhung me; a few shattered pines were scattered around; and the solemn silence of this glorious presence-chamber of imperial Nature was broken only by the brawling waves, or the fall of some vast fragment, the thunder sound of the avalanche, or the cracking reverberating along the mountains of the accumulated ice, which, through the silent working of immutable laws, was ever and anon rent and torn, as if it had been but a plaything in their hands. These sublime and magnificent scenes afforded me the greatest consolation that I was capable of receiving. They elevated me from all littleness of feeling; and although they did not remove my grief, they subdued and tranquillised it. In some degree, also, they diverted my mind from the thoughts over which it had brooded for the last month. I retired to rest at night; my slumbers, as it were, waited on and ministered to by the assemblance of grand shapes which I had contemplated during the day. They congregated round me; the unstained snowy mountain-top, the glittering pinnacle, the pine woods, and ragged bare ravine; the eagle, soaring amidst the clouds – they all gathered round me, and bade me be at peace.

Frankenstein, **Mary Shelley**

QUOTE UNQUOTE

Never ride when you can walk.
BILL GALE, writer

STRIKE A LIGHT

Approximately 50 people in Britain are struck by lightning each year, (no 'they're getting fed up with it' jokes, please). Three of these, on average, are fatal. America has about 75 strikes a year, despite having a much larger surface area.

The figures vary quite remarkably. In 1982, lightning killed 14 people whereas there were no deaths in 2000 and 2001. The last year, prior to 2000, without a single death caused by lightning in Britain was 1937.

There are about 300,000 lightning ground strikes a year in Britain. On average someone is struck every 6,000 strikes, and killed every 100,000 strikes.

A typical thunderstorm will produce 10,000 strikes in a day, but this number can rise to as much as 85,000, as the thunderstorm on 24th July 1994 proved.

29 BENEFITS OF WALKING

Improved efficiency of your heart and lungs

Increased body fat burn

Raised metabolism so you are burning calories faster, even while you rest

Helps to control your appetite

Increased levels of energy

Helps relieve stress

Slows the ageing process

Reduced levels of cholesterol in your blood

Lowers high blood pressure

Helps to control and prevent non-insulin dependent diabetes

Reduced risk of some forms of cancer including colorectal, prostate, and breast

Aids rehabilitation from heart attack and stroke

Promotes intestinal regularity

Helps promote restful sleep

Strengthens your leg muscles, hips, and torso

Strengthens your bones and reduces loss of bone density in older women

Reduces any stiffness in your joints from inactivity or arthritis

Relieves many chronic backache problems

Improved flexibility

Improved posture

Promotes healthier skin resulting from increased circulation

Improved mental alertness and memory

Prompts intellectual creativity and problem solving

Improves your mood

Helps to prevent and/or reduce depression

Improved self-esteem

Increased sexual vigour

Helps to control addictions to nicotine, alcohol, caffeine, and other drugs

Stops you watching so much television

QUOTE UNQUOTE

An early morning walk is a blessing for the whole day.
HENRY DAVID THOREAU, US writer and naturalist

MAD FOR WALKING

44-year-old father-of-two, Stephen Gough, was arrested on numerous occasions on his epic Land's End to John O'Groats journey. The reason? Throughout the walk, he wore only a hat and boots. A human rights activist from Eastleigh in Hampshire, the aim of his adventure was to assert man's right to walk unclothed. Gough repeatedly spent up to a week in prison, accused variously of public order offences, of being in possession of a knife, and of indecent exposure. Where he kept the knife is a matter for speculation.

THE PRIVATE LIFE OF THE MIDGE

Do not read this if you've just started your dinner.

These little gnats have tormented walkers in the Scottish Highlands as far back as history can recall, and despite countless attempts to get rid of them, they still return with voracious force each year. Midges, as you are probably aware, deliver a bite that is by all means out of proportion to their size. Considering this, in the right conditions for larval development, a hectare of land can contain up to 24 million larvae. In fact, densities have been known to reach around 500,000 in an area 2 metres by 2 metres. Midges can quite rapidly and easily be carried for over a kilometre in the wind, landing on vegetation, tree trunks or unsuspecting prey.

Considering that 60% of a midge's life revolves around reproduction, such great numbers are not surprising. Male midges will form huge swarms in response to the stimulating melody of beating female wings. After copulation, the female midge requires a strict diet of blood for the eggs to develop fully. Red deer blood is the favoured choice due to its availability, although the blood of other mammals, including our own precious droplets, offers a perfectly palatable meal to the female midge.

Midges have highly developed olfactory senses that can detect several chemicals in mammalian body odour. The female midge is attracted by dark coloured, moving objects surrounded by carbon dioxide that is exhaled in the breath of mammals. Once the midge is safely settled on the skin surface of its prey, it begins cutting through the skin with specially developed mouthparts. Once blood is located, the mouthparts are rolled into a sucking tube and inserted into the wound. When swollen with blood, the female releases a pheromone to attract other females. This is what we experience when attacked by a swarm of 2,000 hungry females.

HOW TO DEAL WITH BLISTERS

Blisters are simply the result of friction, but they can make a walk a miserable experience. To help prevent blisters:

* Wear comfortable, good-fitting, worn-in boots or shoes, especially when taking long walks.
* Wear good walking socks in the right size; consider wearing two pairs.
* Keep your toenails trim.
* Change your socks daily.
* Quickly remove any foreign bodies from your socks and boots.
* Ensure that the tongue and laces of your boots are arranged correctly and evenly.
* Check your feet carefully and regularly for any sign of rubbing and tenderness.
* Walk as much as possible in your boots so that hard skin develops at friction points.
* Act immediately you feel any friction or discomfort: blisters can form very quickly.

If you feel a blister developing, stop walking, take your boots and socks off and examine your feet.

Consider applying some material cushioning or padding, or a breathable waterproof plaster, or possibly some strips of surgical tape.

There is some controversy over how to treat blisters when they do occur. Some walkers prefer to burst the blister carefully and immediately apply a sterile dressing. Others argue this runs the risk of infection, and recommend keeping the area clean and protected instead.

Chemists and outdoor shops now supply a wide range of foot care products, including blister kits with 'second skin' dressings providing cushioning from further friction. Use according to the manufacturer's instructions.

WALKING WORDS

One bright day in the last week of February, I was walking in the park, enjoying the threefold luxury of solitude, a book, and pleasant weather; for Miss Matilda had set out on her daily ride, and Miss Murray was gone in the carriage with her mamma to pay some morning calls. But it struck me that I ought to leave these selfish pleasures, and the park with its glorious canopy of bright blue sky, the west wind sounding through its yet leafless branches, the snow-wreaths still lingering in its hollows, but melting fast beneath the sun, and the graceful deer browsing on its moist herbage already assuming the freshness and verdure of spring – and go to the cottage of one Nancy Brown.

Agnes Grey, Anne Bronte

QUOTE UNQUOTE

I was the only kid who anybody I knew has ever seen actually walk into a lamppost with his eyes wide open. Everybody assumed that there must be something going on inside, because there sure as hell wasn't anything going on on the outside!
DOUGLAS ADAMS, novelist

9 REAL ALES PREFERRED BY WALKERS

While a number of ramblers may well sport the beard so beloved of the stereotypical real ale drinker, they tend not to wear the sandals. Such footwear is asking for trouble on stony passes and craggy peaks. But walkers remain ardent real ale aficionados. After all, what better to quench the thirst brought on by a day's map reading than a tepid pint of the brown stuff? Here's a selection of ramblers' favourite brews and the breweries that provide them, as recommended by walking members of CAMRA.

'Firedog' / 'Black Lurcher', The Abbeydale Brewery, Sheffield, South Yorkshire.

Greene King 'Abbot Ale', Greene King Brewing Company, Bury St. Edmunds, Suffolk.

Jennings 'Cumberland Ale', Jennings Brewery, Cockermouth, Cumbria.

Hydes 'Jekyll's Gold', Hydes Brewery, Manchester.

'Sharp's Special', Sharp's Brewery, Rock, Waldebridge, Cornwall.

Greene King 'IPA', Greene King Brewing Company, Bury St. Edmunds, Suffolk.

Whim Hartington 'IPA', Whim Brewery, Hartington, Derbyshire.

'Ringwood Best', Ringwood Brewery, Ringwood, Hampshire.

'Old Brewery Bitter', Samuel Smith's Brewery, Tadcaster, North Yorkshire.

And one to watch out for...
'Rambler's Ruin', The Breconshire Brewery, Brecon, Powys.

A MAN WALKS INTO A BAR...

... with a dog. 'This dog is the smartest dog in the world,' he says. 'He can answer any question.' 'Oh yeah?' says the barman. 'Prove it!' The man turns to his dog, and asks, 'What is above our head?' 'Roof!' 'How does bark feel?' 'Ruff!' 'Give me a girl's name.' 'Ruth!' The other drinkers, growing tired of the show, throw the man and his dog out of the bar. The dog turns to the man and asks, 'Should I have said Elizabeth?'

Percentage of Australian walkers who are female 67

Claude Duvall

Duvall was born in Normandy in 1643 and came to England as the Duke of Richmond's footman in 1660. Famous for his fashionable dress, gentleman's manners and gallant treatment of the ladies, he was renowned for stopping coaches at Holloway, on the road between Islington and Highgate in North London. His reputation for being a ladies' man grew after he danced with one while her husband, who had just given up £100, looked on helplessly. Captured in the Hole in the Wall pub in Chandos Street, London, he was hanged in 1670, despite many ladies of the court apparently intervening to plea for his life.

John Nevison

Known as 'Swift Nick' for his famous 200-mile cross-country escape in 1676, John Nevison is thought to have been born in Pontefract in 1639 and worked as an exciseman before turning to highway robbery – attacking the coaches of the Great North Road between Huntingdon and York. The 200-mile dash took place after a 4am robbery in Kent when Nevison apparently rode up to York in time for sunset the same day, where he dropped in on a game of bowls with the Mayor. The Mayor's testimony enabled him to evade arrest and he continued on the highways until he was captured at Sandal, and hanged in 1684.

Dick Turpin

One of England's most famous highwaymen, Dick Turpin has probably erroneously been credited for John Nevison's famous escape from Kent to York. Born in 1705 in Essex, Turpin trained as a butcher in Whitechapel who turned to cattle rustling to increase his profits. A member of the 'Essex Gang' he robbed remote farmhouses and held up carriages in Epping Forest. When it became too hot to remain in Essex, he changed his name and moved to Yorkshire where he was soon arrested and imprisoned in York Castle. It was only by a series of coincidences that he was identified as Dick Turpin – by his former schoolmaster who recognised his handwriting on a letter sent to his brother. He was hanged at York in 1739.

James Maclaine

Born in 1724, the son of a Scottish Minister, Maclaine started a life of crime after gambling away his father's fortune. Pairing up with a William Plunkett, a bankrupt apothecary, they decided to rob the rich and famous – holding up carriages in Hyde Park – with some style. After accidentally shooting Horace Walpole – son of Sir Robert Walpole – he wrote him a letter of apology. Caught while trying to sell Lord Eglington's coat, Maclaine was hanged in 1750.

MORE POTENTIAL RAMBLING ANTHEMS

Walking In My Shoes
Depeche Mode

The Walk – The Cure

The Walk – Eurythmics

Walking On Broken Glass
Annie Lennox

Walking On Thin Ice
Yoko Ono

Walking With A Zombie
Army of Lovers

Strollin' – Prince

Walking In The Sunshine
Bad Manners

Walking Down Your Street
Bangles

Walking Distance – Buzzcocks

Walk Right Back
Everly Brothers

Walking In Memphis
Cher

HELLO AND GOODBYE

Five mammals you wouldn't have encountered while out walking in
Britain 300 years ago...
1. Coypu . . . . first known in the wild 1930s
2. American mink . . . . first known in the wild 1930s
3. Chinese muntjac . . . . first known in the wild 1920s
4. Grey squirrel . . . . first known in the wild 1876
5. Brown rat. . . . . first known in the wild 1720s

...and five mammals you're unlikely to encounter today
1. Coypu. . . . . last known in the wild 1987
2. Wolf . . . . last known in the wild 1690s
3. Lynx . . . . last known in the wild 300 AD
4. Elk . . . . last known in the wild 2000 BC
5. Woolly mammoth . . . . last known in the wild 10,800 BC

THE SAXON WAYS

*Two types of road were referred to during Saxon times: herepaths (used
by armies) and portways (trading paths that led to markets and ports).*

Known Saxon Routes

From	To	Type
Shaftesbury	Salisbury (The Salisbury Way)	Herepath
Marlborough	Avebury (The Wiltshire Herepath)	Herepath
Northampton	Southampton	Portway
Silchester	Old Sarum	Portway
Nottingham	Bakewell	Portway

Unfortunately (for the rambler, at any rate), the builder is apt to put out of gear to-day the walk that was prepared yesterday, so that occasionally ramblers, instead of merrily henting the stile-a, may have to cover a bit of concrete road lined with villas or to steer round a clot of bungalows before being able to jog on along the footpath again. Such incidentals of progress, however, the good rambler takes in his stride. At the same time, it would be helpful if he dropped a postcard to the Publicity Officer of London Transport, drawing attention to uncharted shoals of this sort.

Recent legislation concerning rights of way is reflected by the erection of guideposts at the extremities of public footpaths, the Essex County Council in particular being prominent in this good work. Contrariwise, land owners or occupiers have in a few instances sought to debar the public from fieldpaths, even church paths, that have been used since time out of memory. There is nothing new in this. The writer has by him a record of a certain John Aas being charged with obstructing a footpath at Reigate in 1333. That path may be in use to-day.

Generally farmers and land-owners respect rights of way across their property, and every good rambler should return the compliment by closing gates after him and keeping to the path. The more the farmer and the townsman come into contact with each other the better it must be for both. The farmer's problems will be better understood, and the Londoner may even find interest in the Fat Stock Prices of the Six o'Clock News.

Country Walks, published by **London Transport**, 1937

RAMBLING RIDDLE

I was walking down Mulberry Lane,
I met a man doing the same.
He tipped his hat and drew his cane,
And in this rhyme I said his name.
What was the man's name? Answer on page 153.

HOW IT ALL BEGAN

The idea for the Pennine Way came after two young American correspondents wrote to Tom Stephenson, then the outdoor correspondent of the Daily Herald, to ask if Britain had anything similar to the USA's 2,500-mile Appalachian Trail. In an article dated June 22, 1935, Tom, who later became the first director of the Ramblers' Association, came up with the idea of a 'long green trail' between the Peak and the Cheviots, 'which the feet of grateful pilgrims would, with the passing years, engrave on the face of the land'.

70   *Percentage of energy cut from walking when wearing motorised petrol boots*

MAP READING FOR
THE COUNTRYGOER

THE RAMBLERS' ASSOCIATION
TWO SHILLINGS

*Bill was beginning to wish he had a copy of
'Map reading for the guy-who-wants-to-go-back-home-again'.*

10 LONGEST SIGNED TRAILS IN THE UK

1. South West Coast Path: 630 miles from Minehead in Somerset to South Haven Point near Poole, Dorset.

2. Monarch's Way: 610 miles from Worcester to Shoreham (Sussex).

3. Ulster Way: 570 miles, a circular route from Belfast taken in an anti-clockwise direction.

4. Macmillan Way network: 435 miles from Boston (Lincs) to Abbotsbury or Barnstaple (Devon).

5. Pennine Bridleway: 350 miles from Middleton Top (Derbys) to Byrness (Northumberland).

6. Trans Pennine Trail: 350 miles (560 km) from Southport (Manchester) to Chesterfield, Leeds, York or Hornsea.

7. Pennine Way: 268 miles (429 km) from Edale in the Peak District to Kirk Yetholm in the Scottish Borders.

8. Midshires Way: 225 miles (362 km) from Bledlow or Great Kimble (Bucks) to Stockport.

9. Hardy Way: 214 miles (343 km) from Higher Bockhampton to Stinsford Church, Dorset.

10. Southern Upland Way: 212 miles (341 km) from Portpatrick to Cockburnspath in Scotland.

HOW DOES A THERMOS FLASK WORK?

All a thermos flask is doing is limiting heat transfer through the walls of the thermos. It lets the fluid inside the thermos keep its temperature nearly constant for a long period of time (whether the temperature is hot or cold).

The Foam Thermos Flask
Foam is a poor heat conductor and the air inside the foam is an even worse heat conductor, therefore making heat almost impossible to wriggle in or out. You can make your own thermos flask by wrapping a jar in foam insulation.

The Vacuum Thermos Flask
A vacuum is a lack of atoms. A 'perfect vacuum' contains zero atoms. It is nearly impossible to create a perfect vacuum, but you can get close. Without atoms you eliminate conduction and convection completely.

If you look inside your thermos you will see a mirrored sheet of glass. Around this glass is a vacuum which creates a fragile glass envelope. It is protected by a plastic or metal casing. The glass is silvered (like a mirror) to reduce infrared radiation. The combination of a vacuum and the silvering greatly reduces heat transfer by convection, conduction and radiation, which in turn keeps your tea warm and your juice cool. Not at the same time, though.

QUOTE UNQUOTE

The ghost that got into our house on the night of November 17, 1915, raised such a hullabaloo of misunderstandings that I am sorry I didn't just let it keep on walking, and go to bed.
JAMES THURBER, humorist

WALKING WORDS

On Tuesday I received a note from Jack Toledano asking me to meet him today at the Star and Garter in Putney at the usual time. I am used to these notes. Jack does not need to specify the time. If I cannot make it he goes for a walk himself, but I always try to be there because there is nothing better than going for a walk with Jack Toledano. London is a walker's paradise, he says, but you have to know where to go. Paris is for the flaneur, he says, but London is for the walker. The only way to think, he says, is at a desk, the only way to talk is on a walk.

Gabriel Josipovici, writer, *Moo Pak*

20 COLLECTIVE ANIMAL NAMES

A clutter...of cats
A brood ....of chickens
A parliament..of owls
An unkindness ....of ravens
A shulk ....of foxes
A tribe ....of goats
A bevy ....of swans
A swine ....of pigs
A flight ....of bees
A deceit..of lapwings
A siege...of herons
A murder ....of crows
A pod ....of seals
A storytelling ....of rooks
A scurry...of squirrels
A murmuration..of starlings
A hover ....of trout
A generation ....of vipers
A nest...of hornets
A nide...of pheasants

HERE TO ETERNITY

A fastish walking speed is three miles in one hour on the flat, taking roughly twenty minutes per mile. Based on this information, it would take...

17 hours to walk from London to Brighton (50 miles)

17 days to walk from John O'Groats to Land's End (1209 miles)

7 weeks to walk from London to New York (3470 miles)

10 weeks to walk from London to Beijing (5071 miles)

10 years to walk from London to the Moon (239,000 miles)

3,844 years to walk from London to the Sun (93,000,000 miles)

99,000 years to walk from London to Proxima Centauri (24,000,000,000,000 miles)

WALKING AND BRAS

In October 1999 two women were killed by a bolt of lightning while out walking in Hyde Park. The women were both wearing underwired bras that acted as lightning conductors.

WALKER'S LAWS? MURPHY'S LAWS

There are no short cuts to any place worth going.

Licensing hours are the times of the day when no pub is in sight.

Any stone in your boot always travels to exactly the point of most pressure.

The weight of your pack increases in proportion to the amount of food you consume from it.

The horizon remains constant as soon as darkness begins to fall.

The number of stones in your boot correlates to the number of hours you have been walking.

The hardest trail markers to find are the most important.

Look before you leap, but remember that he who hesitates is lost.

The net weight of your boots is proportional to the cube of the number of hours you have been on the trail.

Destinations are always full on arrival. Yet when you phone ahead, there is no-one to answer.

When you take your boots off, they become two sizes smaller.

Socks come to life when the foot is booted.

LONG WAY TO GO

The longest recorded walk around the British Isles was completed by John Westley of Kessingland, Suffolk, England who walked 9,469 miles around the British Isles, starting on August 5th 1990 and finishing on September 20th 1991. His walk began and ended at Tower Bridge, London.

A FRIEND IN NEED

Two men were travelling together, when a bear suddenly met them on their path. One of them climbed up quickly into a tree and concealed himself in the branches. The other, seeing that he must be attacked, fell flat on the ground, and when the bear came up and felt him with his snout, and smelt him all over, he held his breath, and feigned the appearance of death as much as he could. The bear soon left him, for it is said he will not touch a dead body. When he was quite gone, the other traveller descended from the tree, and jocularly inquired of his friend what it was the bear had whispered in his ear. 'He gave me this advice,' his companion replied. 'Never travel with a friend who deserts you at the approach of danger.'

Aesop, *Fables*

THE WALKER'S WALKER

The man behind Wainwright's Walks
'One should always have a definite objective, in a walk as in life.'

The son of a stonemason; born and bred in the face of poverty in Blackburn, Lancashire; a school leaver at 13. A man of such modest means could never have guessed that his habit of wandering through the countryside and mountains would turn into a career that would make him one of the most famous outdoors writers of all time.

Yet Alfred Wainwright ended his days with about 50 publications to his name on walking, the pleasures of walking, and walking discoveries. He had become the walker's walker.

It was at the age of 23, when he took a week's holiday to the Lake District, that his interest turned into a devotion. 'I was utterly enslaved by all I saw', he later wrote in one of his greatest works, his self-confessed 'love letter', *The Pictorial Guides to the Lakeland Fells*, which spanned seven volumes and took 13 years to write.

While AW, as he is affectionately known, first found fame and respect with the publication of his *Lakeland Fells Guides*, it was his aptly named *A Coast to Coast Walk*, for which he is probably best remembered today.

The walk is a 190-mile trek from the West Coast of England to the East, which he first paced out between 1970 and 1971. His meticulously detailed recording of the journey is used to this day. starting at St. Bee's in Cumbria on the coast of the Irish Sea, the trail twists and turns through the Lake District, the Limestone country, the Yorkshire Dales and the North York Moors, to the end point at Robin Hood's Bay on the North Sea. Two thirds of the walk covers three national parks, ensuring that the journey is rich in scenery, geographical history and beautiful wildlife.

The walk takes about 12 days, varying on each individual and their levels of fitness and keenness. Some walkers break the walk up, taking on small chunks at weekends and perhaps taking years to complete.

Yet however you tackle the journey, there's an established custom you might like to follow. Pick up a stone from the Irish Sea as you set off, and once you reach the North Sea, drop it in. Whether it's taken you 12 days or 12 years to finish the entire trip, it'll be a symbolic moment for you as you complete for the first time Wainwright's most famous walk.

Man is not man sitting down: he is man on the move.
STEPHEN GRAHAM, journalist

10 WORST CROSSINGS IN BRITAIN

1 **Suffolk at Washbrook** where the A12 and A14 merge (GR 124422). Several footpaths converge at this spot. The crossing here, if anybody was foolhardy enough to attempt it, would mean the user would have to negotiate 12 lanes of high volume speeding traffic.

2 **Sheffield at Catcliffe** where a footpath and a footway cross the A630 (GR 406878). The sheer volume and speed of the traffic makes this crossing an accident blackspot.

3 **Hampshire at Hordle** where a byway crosses the A337 (GR 279938). The crossing point suffers from poor visibility due to a hedge and an adverse bend creating a high-risk crossing.

4 **Surrey at Send** where a footpath crosses the A3 (GR 031540). A veritable triple whammy here. High volume of traffic travelling at fast speeds compounded by poor visibility. One of many dangerous crossings on the A3 but in the Ramblers' Association's opinion the worst.

5 **Cambridgeshire at Conington** where a footpath is severed by the A14 (GR 331675). This is another road that carries dense and fast-moving traffic and is very dangerous to cross.

6 **Dorset at Wootton Fitzpaine** where three footpaths meet the A35 (GR 342952), including the Wessex Ridgeway and the Liberty Trail. Speed and poor visibility make this crossing very dangerous.

7 **Derbyshire at Borrowash** where a footpath crosses the A52 (GR 415354). Once again the lethal combination of high volume and high speed makes this crossing extremely hazardous.

8 **East Riding at Bilton** where the A165 splits the hamlet (GR 148341): a high volume, high speed, poor visibility location.

9 **West Sussex at Slaugham** where 2 footpaths cross the A23 (GR 265275). The A23 has many problem crossings caused by the high volume and speed of the traffic. The problem is twice as bad here as two footpaths cross at the same point.

10 **Dorset at Winterbourne Abbas** where a bridleway and minor road cross the A35 at a bend (GR 589907). The same old story of high volume, high speed and poor visibility.

CAN ALSO BE USED FOR...

Bandana	Napkin, washcloth, headband, bandage, towel, hat, scarf, water filter, water collector or fire starter.
Cord	Clothing line, to tie extras to your backpack, to lower a water bottle into a hard reaching water source, to lower your gear down a steep cliff, to stretch out a tent or to make an animal line (see page 40).
Walking stick	Rake to smooth ground before erecting tent, to wave aggressively at angry farm dogs, to flick debris off the trail, to fight back overgrown vegetation, to probe the ground for snakes or to attach a cloth and turn it into a sunshade during lunchtime.
Baking soda	Toothpaste, boot deodorizer, underarm deodorant or to soak your feet in after long day.
Cheesecloth	Water filter, bandage, mosquito net, coffee/tea filter or fishing net.

MAD FOR WALKING

Spud Talbot-Ponsonby's 4,500-mile journey around the entire British coastline with her loyal dog, Tess, raised £40,000 for the homeless charity Shelter. She published her travelogue, covering ten months, under the title *Two Feet, Four Paws: The Girl Who Walked Her Dog 4,500 Miles*.

Two years later, Spud found herself confronted by perhaps a new challenge, that of single motherhood. More trials were in store, however: four months following the birth of her baby, she was diagnosed with cervical cancer, for which she needed a radical hysterectomy. Spud tackled this difficult period in her life by setting off on another walking trip, her route now following the old drove roads of Scotland from Aberlour to Blairgowrie. Again accompanied by Tess, she had further companions in the shape of her new partner, and baby who rode in a basket on top of Ben, Spud's carthorse. This time she managed to raise £4,000 for Maggie's Centre, an Edinburgh support centre for young women with cancer. Spud's book, *Small Steps with Heavy Hooves* is based on these experiences.

RAMBLING RIDDLE

Unravel the following:
roforkad
Answer on page 153

10 PHYSICAL BANES OF A WALKER'S LIFE

Callouses ● Achilles tendonitis ● Heel bursitis
Hammer toes ● Corns ● Chilblains
Haglunds heel bumps ● Cracked dry heels
Foot ulcers ● Sweaty feet

THE WAY THROUGH THE WOODS

They shut the road through the woods
Seventy years ago.
Weather and rain have undone it again,
And now you would never know
There was once a path through the woods
Before they planted the trees,
It is underneath the coppice and the heath,
And the thin anemones.
Only the keeper sees
That, where the ring-dove broods,
And the badgers roll at ease,
There was once a road through the woods.

Yet, if you enter the woods
Of a summer evening late,
When the night-air cools on the trout-ring'd pools
Where the otter whistles his mate,
(They fear not men in the woods
Because they see so few)
You will hear the beat of a horse's feet
And the swish of a skirt in the dew,
Steadily cantering through
The misty solitudes,
As though they perfectly knew
The old lost road through the woods...
But there is no road through the woods.
Rudyard Kipling, *The Way through the Woods*

SEXUAL PLEASURES THAT WALKERS
MIGHT ENJOY

Urtication is the stimulation of the skin by stinging nettles. Its original use was to help bring sensation back to paralysed limbs, but some like to use nettles for sexual stimulation, wearing them inside underwear, or applying to the penis before putting on a condom to compensate for the sensation lost by the latex barrier.

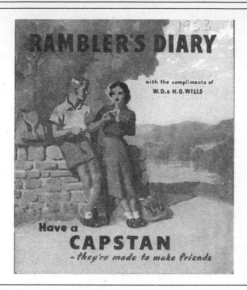

In 1953, cigarette-makers WD & HO Wills published a small Rambler's Diary. In amongst titbits of information on what natural delights each month might offer, they published the following advice: *Insect bites. Keep the insects away with Dimethylphthalate – show this word to a chemist and ask him for a prescription containing it. Another good remedy: smoke a Capstan or a Woodbine.*

WALK TO SCHOOL DAY

The first British Walk to School week took place in Hertfordshire, with only a small number of schools participating. In 1995, Living Streets (then called the Pedestrians Association) began its involvement with the scheme, and the week became a national event. In 1997, Chicago and Los Angeles took up the idea. Canada did the same in 1998, with Ireland and New Zealand joining in 1999. At this time the events were run separately, but in October 2000, more than 2.5 million walkers in seven countries took part in the first International Walk to School Day. In Britain, the world's longest 'walking bus', at over a quarter of a mile in length, ferried pupils to a school in Dorset. Further International Walk to School Days have been organised each October since then, with the number of participating countries growing all the time.

John E Walker b.1941
Chemist who shared the Nobel prize for chemistry for his contribution towards the elucidation of the enzymatic mechanism underlying the synthesis of adenosine triphosphate. But you already knew that.

William B Walker
American businessman who took the thermos flask to America after seeing it in Berlin in 1906.

Lewis Walker
American business partner of Whitcomb Judson. Together they helped develop the modern zipper from an original design to replace shoelaces on boots.

John Walker
One of the first owners of *Cosmopolitan* magazine, Walker introduced the idea of 'dignified sensationalism' and made the magazine a success by the early 20th century.

Craven Walker
British inventor of the lava lamp. Walker developed the lamp from a liquid-filled lamp he saw in a pub in post WWII England. His design took off during the psychedelic movement of the 60s when sales soared.

Madame CJ Walker 1867-1919
An American businesswoman who developed hair products for African-American women. She was thought to be the first American self-made millionairess.

Johnnie Walker
BBC Radio 2 disc jockey who made his name on Radio Caroline in the 1960s. He went on to present the Radio 2 drive time show.

Walker Evans
American photographer who became famous for his documentation of the Depression in his book *Let us now praise famous men*.

AB Walker
Mayor of Liverpool and major financier of the Walker Art Gallery. He contributed a total of about £60,000 to enable the museum to be opened in 1877.

A LOAD OF COBBLERS...

... is called a drunkship.
The word cobbler is more properly applied to shoe repairmen. Those who actually make footwear are known as 'cordwainers'. This term has its antecedents in the word 'cordovan' which was a reddish leather produced in Spain. Hence, one who worked in cordovan was a cordwainer. Cobble comes from the middle English word cobel – a stone. To cobble, as a verb, means to make a makeshift repair.

Shortly after the death of his father, killed by Oliver Cromwell who by then ruled England, King Charles II landed in Scotland from France, where he was crowned king of England.

He managed to raise an army in little time and marched south with the intention of defeating Cromwell and restoring the monarchy.

Charles met Cromwell at Worcester on 3rd September, 1651, and so followed the battle of Worcester. Cromwell's army defeated Charles, leaving his men wounded and dying. The king, with his most trusted aides, including Lords Wilmot and Derby, rode north to the border of Shropshire and Staffordshire, deep in the Brentwood Forest.

Six weeks of hot pursuit followed, with the king's concealment across England. A reward of £1000, (equivalent to 30 years' wages of the average musketeer) was offered by Cromwell for the king's head.

On 15 October, he reached the south coast, narrowly avoiding capture, and took passage from Shoreham to Frecamp in France, where he stayed until the restoration of the monarchy two years after Cromwell's death in 1658.

Today, the Monarch's Way is a long distance walk stretching over 610 miles, along footpaths and bridleways closely following the route taken by Charles. It begins in Worcester and finishes in Shoreham.

5 WALKING PHRASES THAT AREN'T ABOUT WALKING...

Take a hike
Walk the plank
Walk off into the sunset
Walk on the wild side
Take a long walk off a short pier

...AND 5 FOOT PHRASES THAT AREN'T ABOUT FEET

Best foot forward
Get your foot in the door
Get your feet wet
One foot in the grave
Keep your feet on the ground

QUOTE UNQUOTE

I dream of hiking into my old age. I want to be able even then to pack my load and take off slowly but steadily along the trail.
MARILYN DOAN, writer

5 WAYS OF DEALING WITH DOG POO WITHOUT USING A POOP-A-SCOOP

Get your dog to eat dung beetles – every time the dog poos, the dung beetles that emerge will deal with it.

Invent some dog poo detector shoes with GPS tracking to warn other walkers.

Walk behind a caninette – one of France's motorcycle dog poo vacuum cleaners. There are 75 of them in Paris and they each suck up 110lb of dog poo a day.

Get a dog nappy – remember, different shapes fit different breeds.

Feed your dog with bioluminescent dog food so that its poo shows up in the dark. As an added bonus, it could save on street lighting too.

INTERESTED IN POTENTIAL RAMBLING ANTHEMS? TRY THESE

Walking Song – Turtles

Walk on by – Burt Baccarach

I walk the line – Johnny Cash

Walk this world – Heather Nova

Walking Town – Jackson Browne

Walk on – U2

Walk song – Blind Melon

Walk right in – Janis Joplin

Walking back to happiness
Helen Shapiro

Superman can't walk
Good Charlotte

Walking the Dog
Rufus Thomas

Walk Away Renee
Vonda Shepherd

A TRUNK ROUTE

After an eight-hour hill walk, the average walker will have carried a weight on his or her hips and knee joints equivalent to that of 62 full-grown African elephants.

The Wildlife and Countryside Act makes it illegal to have a bull at large in a field containing a public path if it belongs to one of the dairy breeds. But, if the bull is not more than ten months old, or if it belongs to a beef breed and is with cows or heifers, it is legal.

Below you can see the possible beef breeds of bull you might encounter while out on your walks. After all, it's always useful to know what might be chasing you.

If the bull that has tossed you over the fence doesn't appear to be listed below, turn to page 92, where you might find it among the dairy breeds.

This chart is reproduced by permission of the Ramblers' Association and *The Countryman*, in which it first appeared.

Lincoln Red Reddish brown

BEEF BREEDS

Hereford Tan with white face

South Devon Brown

Charolais Pale cream

Beef Shorthorn Brown

Aberdeen Angus Black

Welsh Black Black

A BUDDING ATHLETE

Zola Budd is mainly remembered for controversy and bare feet. The young South African broke Mary Decker's record for the 5000m in January 1984 but the time was not recognised as South Africa had been banned from international sporting events because of its policy of apartheid. However, Budd was determined to compete at the 1984 Olympics in Los Angeles and so encouraged by her father she applied for British citizenship on the grounds that she had a British grandfather. The Daily Mail supported her claim and it was rapidly granted. She was duly selected for the British Olympic team and was selected for the 3000m. Mary Decker was the home town favourite and expected to win. However, after 1700m the two athletes collided and Decker fell and did not complete the race. Budd was booed for the rest of the race and eventually finished seventh. She continued to compete and in 1988 moved back to South Africa. She nearly always ran in bare feet, claiming that she found it more comfortable than wearing spikes.

WALKING THE PLANK

The mythical status of walking the plank owes more to Peter Pan and pirate films than to reality. Men were certainly thrown overboard to finish them off, but walking the plank was not considered to give enough entertainment when there were other varied forms of torture open to the pirates such as lighting matches between their toes or throwing bottles at them. Who'd be a pirate, eh?

7 TYPES OF PURPRESTURE

Marker stones or boulders, with or without mowing of verge.

Mowing of verge, with or without planting of shrubs.

Mowing of verge and barrier stones along edge of tarmac.

Mowing of verge and semi-temporary posts and chain.

Permanent walling, hedging or fencing.

Cultivation of highway verge up to the edge of tarmac.

Building on a highway or a common.

In case you're still wondering, purpresture is a wrongful encroachment upon, or enclosure of, another's property, especially property that should be common or public, such as rivers, harbours and common land.

WALKING WORDS

Every day at Down my father used to take us for the most romantic walks, telling us stories about the places as we went: up the steep hill to Cudham Church; or to look for orchids at Orchis Bank, or along a legendary smuggler's track, or to the Big Woods where Uncle William had been lost as a child. The sudden valleys, the red, red earth full of strangely shaped flints, the great lonely woods, the sense of remoteness, made it different from any other place we knew. We were only sixteen miles from London Bridge, and yet it was so quiet that if a cart came down our lane we all rushed to look over the orchard wall to see it go by.

Period Piece, a Cambridge Childhood, Gwen Raverat

LOOK BEHIND YOU

The Oscar-winning actor Alec Guinness trained at the Fay Compton Studio of Dramatic Arts in London but enhanced his skills by following Londoners around and imitating their walks and gestures. Could YOU be the original George Smiley, Obi-wan Kenobi or Man in a White Suit?

8 TIPS FOR WILD COUNTRY CAMPING

In England and Wales wild camping is not legal without the landowner's permission. In Scotland, follow the code issued by the Mountaineering Council for Scotland.

Look for a sheltered site, and try to find a flat, stoneless spot.

Don't camp in a hollow, or too close to a swollen river, and make sure you face your tent away from the prevailing wind.

Organise the inside of the tent for a quick exit in case of emergencies.

Don't cook inside the tent.

Leave wet clothes to dry in the tent porch.

Site your 'toilet' at least 100m metres from water.

Always leave the camp site as you found it.

LONG WAY TO GO

The first to walk to both poles was Robert Swan from the UK who led the three-man 'In the footsteps of Scott' South Pole expedition in 1986, and three years later headed the eight-man 'Icewalk' North Pole Trek.

Year in the 19th century that shoe sizes were standardised in the UK 85

ALL YOU EVER NEEDED TO KNOW
ABOUT THE WALK

Walking has been acknowledged as an Olympic sport since 1956, when the 20km and 50km races were added to its agenda.

The Rules

There are two rules that distinguish racewalking from running or regular walking.

Straight Leg Rule: From the time the leading foot hits the ground until it passes under the centre of the body, the knee must not be bent. If a judge sees a bent knee, the walker is flashed a paddle showing a bent line, and the walker risks disqualification.

Contact Rule: During the period of each step, the advancing foot of the walker must make contact with the ground before the rear foot leaves the ground. This loss of contact must be visible to the naked eye and seen by a judge. A judge shows the walker a paddle with a wavy line on it and the walker risks disqualification. In running, the runner bends his/her knees with the advancing leg and also has a 'flight phase' in each stride where both feet are off the ground at the same time.

The two rules of racewalking ensure that the walker is walking rather than running.

Due to the inflexibility of the rules, it is a common phenomenon for walkers to get disqualified – the only leniency is that a walker is given two warnings (for having broken one of the rules) and on the third is given the 'boot'. In the Sydney 2000 Olympics, the first three racers in the Women's 20km Racewalk were disqualified, all in the last kilometre. Why? All three of these contenders had become momentarily airborne and one by one they were being found out. The third cheat to be revealed burst into tears as she was disqualified within 200 metres of her medal. On being asked what she wanted by a journalist, she morbidly answered that she could do with a gun, with which to shoot herself.

WATER WALKS

LITTLE HAVEN TO BROAD HAVEN, PEMBROKESHIRE

Little Haven is a charming little Pembrokeshire coal-mining village. Heading North East along its beach at low tide, The Settlands is reached. A delightful sandy beach, it offers shelter from the winds thanks to high cliff faces on either side. Rounding the headland known as The Rain on the northern end of The Settlands, the route leads to Broad Haven bay. Broad Haven is a good bathing beach but again can be reached from the other bays only at low tide.

THESE STILTS WERE MADE FOR WALKING

In China around 7 BC, an entertainer named Leizi would perform for the emperor of Song by walking and running atop two wooden poles taller than himself, which were attached to his lower legs. The popularity of stilt-walking has ebbed and flowed since then, but the following feats suggest that everyone in France was doing it in the late 19th century:

1860 Niagara Falls is crossed on stilts by Jean Francois Gravelet, aka Charles Blondin

1891 Sylvain Dornon stilt-walks from Paris to Moscow via Vilno (1,830 miles) in 58 days (31.55 miles a day).

1892 M Garisoain of Bayonne, France stilt-walks the 4.97 miles into Biarritz in 42 minutes (7.1 mph).

1894 The Landes 273-mile stilt race is held in France at an average speed of 4.4 mph.

RAMBLING RIDDLE

Unravel the following:
wo^{KING}ods
Answer on page 153.

6 PLACES CALLED WALKER IN THE US

Walker County, Alabama
Founded in 1823

City of Walker, Michigan
Founded in 1837

Walker, Minnesota
Founded in 1896

Walker County, Georgia
Founded in 1833

Walker Inn
A mid-19th century stagecoach inn situated at Old Valleytown, Carolina

Walker Point, Kennebunkport
Former president George Bush Snr owns a summer house here. Note that the 'dubya' in his similarly presidential son's name stands for Walker

WALKING AND BRAS

The Jogbra was invented in 1977 by Hinda Miller and a friend who made it out of two jockstraps sewn together. Unused jockstraps, that is.

QUOTE UNQUOTE

I may not have gone where I intended to go, but I think I have ended up where I intended to be.
DOUGLAS ADAMS, novelist

HOLY WALKS

The Golden Temple at Cuzco in Peru was for centuries a spiritual centre for the Incas. Every Inca travelled to visit Cuzco at least once in their life to worship the sun and as a result Cuzco became the centre of Inca civilisation.

HOW TO MAKE A MEASURING WHEEL

Measuring wheels are used to measure out precise distances. Most manufactured wheels are expensive so costs can be avoided if you make your own. The easiest way to do this is to buy an old bicycle with wheels that have a diameter of about 20 inches. You will just need to use the front wheel and fork of the bike. The wheel has to be in good shape, and move and rotate freely. Detach the fork from the bike and for the guiding wheel attach either a metal or wood handle, preferably T-shaped. Next attach the odometer, it is best if it reads in feet or hundredths of a mile. Odometers are built for wheels of various diameters and can be purchased at bicycle stores or surveying suppliers.

NINE NICE NAMES

The cutest trail names in Britain
1. Butter Bee Lane
2. Lovers Lane
3. Pott's Delight
4. Possum Poop Patty
5. The Happy Feet
6. Bendy's Bends
7. Pony Shoe
8. Oliver Twist
9. Daffodil Dawdle

QUOTE UNQUOTE

Slow down and enjoy life. It's not only the scenery you miss by going too fast – you also miss the sense of where you are going and why.
EDDIE CANTOR, comedian and singer

WALKING WORDS

In the fifties and sixties, travelling on foot ceased to be a social degradation. The walking-tour became popular. It was not then called hiking, and it never should have been. Hiking suggests a strenuous covering of ground; what they did in the middle of century was the more leisurely stroll. Some of those foot travellers left accounts of their tours, and they make pleasant, quiet reading in these times. The few accounts one has seen of hiking have something of a crowd and clamour about them; they do not convey the spirit of the true walking-tour, the spirit of solitude and calm which arises from the books of the time.

Travel in England, Thomas Burke. On the 19th century.

THE WALKER'S BASIC FIRST AID KIT

10 plasters in various sizes
2 large sterile dressings for severe bleeds
1 medium sterile dressing for large wounds
4 triangular bandages to support suspected broken bones,
dislocations and sprains
1 eye pad in case of cut to the eye
4 safety pins to secure dressings
Disposable gloves for hygiene

10 WALKING ETYMOLOGIES

Ramble	From Middle Dutch, *rammelen*, to wander about in sexual excitement (usually applied to night wanderings of cats); and *rammen*, to copulate.
Walk	From Old English *wealcan*, to roll, toss or wander.
Amble	From Latin *ambulare*, to walk.
Stroll	Probably from German *strolch*, a vagabond.
March	From French *marcher*, to walk.
Blister	From Old French *blestre*, a swelling or pimple.
Rucksack	From German *rucken*, back, and Greek *sakkos*, sack.
Trail	From Latin *tragula*, a dragnet.
Thermos	From Greek *thermo*, hot
Janet Street-Porter	From feminine form of John, meaning 'Gift of God'; Latin *strata*, paved way; Latin *portare*, carry.

GHOSTLY FOOTSTEPS

Jean Clarke claimed a ghost got into her car when she stopped in darkness on the roadside near Borley village to look at a map. Her dog began howling and she turned to the front passenger seat to find it occupied by a man in a long old-fashioned coat. She had not seen or heard the man enter the car. He pointed in the direction she was going and the atmosphere in the car became very cold. Mrs Clarke said she assumed the man wanted a lift so she started the engine, but after 40 yards he motioned her to stop and then floated through the door.

QUOTE UNQUOTE

Walk a day, live a week.
OLD FRENCH PROVERB

LONG WAY TO GO

The first verified walk around the world was by David Kunst (b 1939) who left his hometown of Waseca, Minnesota, USA heading east on 20th June 1970 and arrived back in Waseca from the west on 5th October, 1974. His walk took him through America, Europe, Asia and Australia. Kunst walked 14,450 miles, crossing four continents and 13 countries, wearing out 21 pairs of shoes and walking more than 20 million steps.

RAMBLING RIDDLE

Take off the first letter of a word that means 'walk', and leave another word that means 'walk'.
Answer on page 153.

IMMORTALISED IN CONCRETE

Grauman's Chinese Theatre is one of the most famous theatres in the world. When it was built in 1927, no one expected it to become one of the biggest tourist attractions in Los Angeles, but when silent screen star Norma Talmadge visited the new theatre and accidentally stepped into a pavement of wet cement, it was the beginning of the legendary forecourt, now visited by over four million visitors a year. At any time of the day or night, fans can be found viewing the handprints, footprints and signatures of their favorite stars.

Over 200 movie icons have left their mark in the forecourt.

5 HILL WALKING TERMS YOU'D
ALWAYS JUST PRETENDED TO KNOW

Shouldering
This is the practice of taking a path along a route which is neither around an obstacle, nor straight over the top, thereby keeping effort to a minimum. Barging through, would be another way of putting it. A similar practice is often used by Oxford Street shoppers around Christmas time.

Spindrift
This is the attractive, albeit sometimes uncomfortable presence of dry snow that has been blown into swirls above you. If you see such a plume of snow blowing from a mountain summit, you know the high weather is severe.

Spot height
The height of a particular location marked on a map, such as the summit of a mountain.

Verglas
A thin, transparent coat of ice covering rocks. Extremely slippery and potentially dangerous to walk over. The equivalent of black ice on roads and pavements.

Whiteout
When light conditions are poor, and snow is falling or there's a thick mist, the horizon has a tendency to disappear, the ground and sky merging treacherously. This can not only be confusing to the eye, but to the feet, that might find themselves walking on thin air.

WALKING WORDS

The wood I walk in on this mild May day, with the young yellow-brown foliage of the oaks between me and the blue sky, the white star-flowers and the blue-eyed speedwell and the ground ivy at my feet – what grove of tropic palms, what strange ferns or splendid broad-petalled blossoms, could ever thrill such deep and delicate fibres within me as this home scene? Those familiar flowers, these well-remembered bird-notes, this sky with its fitful brightness, these furrowed and grassy fields, each with a sort of personality given to it by the capricious hedgerows – such things as these are the mother tongue of our imagination, the language that is laden with all the subtle inextricable associations the fleeting hours of our childhood left behind them.

The Mill on the Floss, George Eliot

Your at-a-glance guide to the male members of the dairy class of cattle. It is not legal to keep one of these at large in a field with a public path. Take care!

This chart is reproduced by permission of the Ramblers' Association and *The Countryman*, in which it first appeared.

DAIRY BREEDS

Ayrshire Brown-and-white

British Holstein Black-and-white

British Friesian Black-and-white

Jersey Pale fawn

Dairy Shorthorn Brown-and-white

Kerry Black

Guernsey Fawn or fawn-and-white

HOLY WALKS

For ancient Greeks the oracle at the temple of Apollo at Delphi became famous for answering devotees' questions it was even consulted for advice on affairs of states. Delphi was known as the navel of the world – a spiritual, and geographic centre where thousands came to seek help. In fact so many journeyed to Delphi that oracles, which had been given out once a year, were, by popular demand, increased to once a month. Travellers came to this shrine on Mount Parnassus from Greece, Egypt and Asia Minor.

10 DIRECTORS WITH WALK-ON PARTS
IN OTHER PEOPLE'S FILMS

Barry Levinson was the column salesman in *History of the World part I*.

Stephen Spielberg was the Cook County Clerk in *The Blues Brothers*.

George Lucas was a disgruntled theme park tourist in *Beverley Hills Cop III*.

Roger Corman was an FBI official in *Silence of the Lambs*.

Martin Scorsese appeared as a TV executive in *Quiz Show*.

Quentin Tarantino was the disturbed brother in *From Dusk till Dawn*.

Cecil B de Mille appeared as himself in *Sunset Boulevard*.

French director **François Truffaut** played the scientist who communicated with the aliens in *Close Encounters of the Third Kind*.

David Cronenberg was a man at the lake in *To Die For*.

Oliver Stone played a bum in *The Hand*. Careful how you say that.

MODERN PILGRIMAGES

Via Crucis, (the Way of the Cross), is an annual pilgrimage that retraces Christ's journey to Golgotha. Filipino Catholics, who make up more than 80% of the country, put more emphasis on Good Friday, the day Christ died, in the belief that suffering is as much a part of the salvation that comes at the end. Thousands of devotees from Cebu City and its neighbouring cities and towns form a penitential procession, each wearing appropriate costumes. There are Roman soldiers with their realistic and impressive wear, some on horseback, others on foot, followers of Christ showing fear, shame and seeming hopelessness, and the weeping women of Jerusalem. It is Palo transformed into Jerusalem on Good Friday.

EROTIC FEET

The art of sucking toes is known by foot fetishists as 'shrimping'.

QUOTE UNQUOTE

And did those feet in ancient time
Walk upon England's mountains green?
WILLIAM BLAKE, poet

THE GENTLEMANLY THING TO DO

Long, long ago, there was a golden age of cricket: bowlers – fine men all – only appealed when they knew the batsman was out; fielders – those wisest of fellows – only claimed a catch when they knew they'd taken the ball cleanly; and batsmen, perhaps the noblest of them all, 'walked'.

Walking was, and still just about is, the supreme act of sportsmanship. If, while batting, you get the edge of your bat to the ball before it zips through to the wicket-keeper behind, you are out. You have been caught. Thing is, sometimes the edge is so fine that the umpire cannot detect it, and gives you not out. What do you do? Do you mutter a prayer of thanks to the great umpire in the sky, and bat on, telling yourself that this moment of good fortune will doubtless be outbalanced by countless occasions of foul luck in the future? Or does the truth of the matter nag at your conscience so much that you are forced to tip your cap, announce to the umpire: 'I tickled it, old man', tuck your bat under your arm and march off to gasps of admiration from your sporting colleagues? If you do the latter, you are a 'walker'. Unsurprisingly, there are few walkers in modern professional cricket.

On the other hand, the great WG Grace once had his stumps splattered all over the place by a particularly nippy delivery, and despite all the evidence to the contrary, decided he wasn't out. He replaced the bails, and when asked why by the bowler, announced that 'all these people have come to see me bat, not you bowl.'

Golden age? What golden age?

THE HISTORY OF KENDAL MINT CAKE

Legend has it that a Kendal confectioner, Joseph Wiper, stumbled across mint cake while trying to make glacier mints. After taking his eye off the pan for a minute he noticed that the mixture had started to become cloudy, instead of clear – the foundation of mint cake was born.

Wiper began producing mint cake at his Ferney Green factory in Kendal in 1869. Initially just sold to locals, the product became so successful that it began to spread across the North-East.

Wiper retired to British Columbia, but his great-nephew, Robert, carried on with the business. Realising the energy potential of the cake, he supplied Ernest Shackleton's 1914-1916 Antarctic Expedition and the first Everest Expedition. The legend was born.

MY LEFT FOOT

When David Beckham broke his left foot in April 2002, the nation gasped. Would he now miss the World Cup? Would England's hopes be scuppered? Would we ever be free again? The following chain of events were all we read and listened to:

18 April: Beckham crashes his car but is uninjured – he collides with a policeman in a Ford Focus. Beckham was allowed to drive with his left leg in plaster as he was driving an automatic.

27 April: Ted Beckham, David's father, announces that his son may even be fit by mid-May.

3 May: Manchester United announces that Beckham's foot is healing satisfactorily. The day before, Sven Goran Eriksson says that he thinks personally that David Beckham will be OK.

13 May: David Beckham says that he is running again, but his foot is still a bit sore.

26 May: Beckham runs on the pitch before the 2-2 draw with Cameroon. After the friendly ends Beckham comes back out to a cheering crowd and does some light training, including kicking the ball with his injured foot.

28 May: The foot has healed! Praises are sung, hats flung in the air, Beckham is back. Soon afterwards, England get knocked out by Brazil.

QUOTE UNQUOTE

Us sing and dance, make faces and give flower bouquets, trying to be loved. You ever notice that trees do everything to git attention we do, except walk?
ALICE WALKER, US writer

NOT SO NEPALEASY

Nepalese treks to brag about:

Kathmandu to Namche Bazar	150 miles	15 days
Pokhara to Jomoson	68 miles	6 days
Dumbre to Manang	60 miles	6 days
Kathmandu to Gosainkunda	41 miles	4 days
Pokhara to Annapurna	25 miles	3 days

Number of years that walking has been an Olympic sport by 2003 95

THEN AND NOW

Under the Foot and Mouth Disease Order issued in 1938 by the Ministry of Agriculture: 'An inspector of the Ministry or of the Local Authority may (notwithstanding the existence of any footpath or right of way) prohibit the entry of any person into any field in an infected area by giving notice in writing to the occupier.' Fines of 'several pounds' were recorded for those entering prohibited zones.

In 2001, the then Ministry (MAFF), announced that contravention of the Foot and Mouth Order was an offence under section 73 of the Animal Health Act 1981. People found guilty of such an offence were liable to a fine of up to £5,000.

15 FRIENDLY WALK-ON PARTS

In the late 90s, a small cameo role in the series Friends was the TV equivalent of putting your footprints in Hollywood cement. Here's a sample:

Jay Leno	The One With Mrs. Bing
Jon Lovitz	The One With The Stoned Guy
Helen Hunt	The One With Two Parts – Part One
George Clooney	The One With Two Parts – Part Two
Chrissie Hynde	The One With The Baby On The Bus
Brooke Shields	The One After The Superbowl
Julia Roberts	The One After The Superbowl
Charlie Sheen	The One With The Chickenpox
Isabella Rossellini	The One With Frank Jr
Sarah Ferguson	The One With Ross's Wedding
Susan Sarandon	The One With Joey's New Brain
Denise Richards	The One With Ross And Monica's Cousin
Winona Ryder	The One With Rachel's Big Kiss
Brad Pitt	The One With The Rumour
Alec Baldwin	The One With The Tea Leaves

A MAN WALKS INTO A BAR...

...and sits down next to a man with a dog at his feet.
'Does your dog bite?' he asks.
'No.'
A few minutes later the dog takes a chunk out of his leg.
'I thought you said your dog didn't bite!' the man yells.
'That's not my dog.'

Gentlemen walking with a lady will give her the inner path, unless the outer part of the walk is safer. This move will be made without remark, and the lady will assume whenever the gentleman changes his position that there is a sufficient reason for moving from one side to the other.

A lady in the street or park may not be saluted by a gentleman, unless he has first received a slight bow from the lady. He may then raise his hat with the hand farthest from the lady, bow respectfully and pass on, not stopping to speak under any circumstance, unless the lady pauses in her promenade.

When gentlemen unaccompanied by ladies meet, each will raise his hat very slightly, if they are on such terms as to warrant recognition. They will bow only if the person saluted commands special respect, by reason of advanced years, social rank, or attainments, or having taken holy orders. In every such case a gentleman will raise the hat with the hand farthest from the person saluted, but the head need not be completely uncovered.

When a gentleman is escorting a lady in any public place, it is his duty to insist on carrying any article she may have in her hand, except her parasol when it is being used as a sunshade.

When gentlemen pause to speak to each other on the street, they will, as a matter of course, shake hands and bow, lifting the hat with the left hand at the moment of their clasping the right.

Gentlemen will never smoke when walking with a lady, as although there is no intentional disrespect in smoking, the act may suggest to other persons a lesser regard for the lady.

Gentlemen walking together may use any pace not actually violent or ungraceful; but when accompanying ladies, aged persons, or the weak, they will accommodate themselves to their companions.

Gentlemen will not swing their arms, nor sway their bodies in an ungainly fashion when walking. Ladies are never guilty of any such ungraceful action, and need no counsel in that respect.

Ladies sometimes, though very rarely, walk too quickly on the street. That should be avoided; a message by telephone will generally obviate the necessity for speed at the expense of grace.

Ladies walking on the street are not expected to recognise gentlemen or friends on the other side of the road. To do so would necessitate habits of observation inconsistent with ladylike repose.

From a 19th century journal.

WALKING BIRDS

Although there are several species of flightless, walking birds in the world (including 17 species of penguin), only a few of them are ratites. Ratites differ from the penguins and others in that they lack a bony keel to which flight muscles are attached. Those that have this keel are called carinates, whether or not the flight muscles work.

Most of the world's ratites are long extinct, mainly through hunting – the elephant bird of Madagascar, and the 14-foot moa of New Zealand are two examples. Today we are left with just 10 flightless ratites – the ostrich, three cassowary species, two rhea species, the emu and three species of kiwi.

As ratites get about by walking and running, their main muscles reside in their legs, as opposed to the chest which is where the power of flying birds lies. Unsurprisingly, ratite meat is very big business these days.

QUOTE UNQUOTE

The Cat. He walked by himself, and all places were alike to him.
RUDYARD KIPLING, novelist

PUTTING HIS FEET IN YOUR MOUTH

Tongue-twisters are often used by speech therapists to help their patients get to grip with awkward vowel sounds and repetitive consonants. One of the best known includes the toeses of a Biblical character who had become a bit confused. It also made a fine song and dance routine for Gene Kelly and Donald O'Connor in *Singin' in the Rain*.

Moses supposes his toeses are roses
But Moses supposes erroneously
For nobody's toeses are posies of roses
As Moses supposes his toeses to be

A MAN WALKS INTO A BAR...

...with a crocodile, and asks if the barman serves lawyers. 'Sure do,' replies the barman. 'Good,' says the man. 'A pint of bitter for me, then, and a lawyer for the croc.'

The word 'jay' is an early 20th century American slang term for 'a stupid person, or a simpleton'. To jaywalk, therefore, is to cross or walk in the street without regard for traffic – in particular, to cross against traffic lights.

Jaywalking is an offence in a number of countries, including Switzerland, Australia, Japan, Germany and the US, where on-the-spot fines can be imposed. Yet some countries go a step or two further than mere fines:

Russia – A Russian Orthodox priest recently told parishioners that jaywalking was a sin and that God would frown upon them for crossing the road at a red light. This was partly a reaction to the large number of pensioners who died after flouting the Russian equivalent of the Green Cross Code.

Singapore – Singapore is very strict about what would elsewhere be deemed minor offences. The South-East Asian country imposes huge fines for chewing gum, spitting and littering. It also takes a dim view of jaywalking, which can land offenders with a huge fine and even a jail sentence. Repeat offenders could face six months in jail.

Indonesia – Jaywalkers in Jakarta can find themselves humiliated rather than financially penalised. Men are required to do 10 push-ups on the spot, while female transgressors are ordered to stand on one foot for 10 seconds, touching their left ear with their right hand.

WALKING WITH CAVEMEN

Hominids are the succession of species that gradually resulted in the walking beasts we know, love and play backgammon with today.

Australopithecus ramidus	5 to 4 million years BC
Australopithecus afarensis	4 to 2.7 million years BC
Australopithecus africanus	3.0 to 2.0 million years BC
Australopithecus robustus	2.2 to 1.0 million years BC
Homo habilis	2.2 to 1.6 million years BC
Homo erectus	2 to 0.4 million years BC
Homo sapiens	400,000 to 200,000 years BC
Homo sapiens neandertalensis	200,000 to 30,000 years BC
Homo sapiens sapiens	130,000 years BC to present

QUOTE UNQUOTE

A wanderer is man from birth
MATTHEW ARNOLD, poet

WALK LIKE AN ANIMAL

A fly is able to walk walls, windows and ceilings thanks to adhesive forces between its tarsal pads and the surface, which are stronger than the force of gravity. This is why a ceiling-crawling fly is easier to swat than one on, say, a table: the strength of the force that connects the insect to the ceiling requires greater energy to combat each time a foot is lifted, slowing the fly down.

RISE, TAKE UP THY BED AND WALK

With these words, records the Gospel of St John, the raising of Lazarus was complete, and a man who had been dead for four days opened his eyes and came alive once more. Yet why is Lazarus' story otherwise unrecorded, even by the other gospel writers who apparently ignored such an extraordinary miracle?

Whether or not you believe in such biblical matters, the most fascinating suggestion comes from the early 20th century Biblical scholar, Rudolf Steiner.

Steiner begins by describing the ancient Hebrew initiation rite in which a body lies as if dead for a few days, while its spirit explores the heavens, only to return 'a true Israelite'.

'Christ poured out His power upon Lazarus and Lazarus arose a new man' continues Steiner. 'A word in St. John's Gospel arrests our attention. It is said in the story of the miracle that the Lord 'loved' Lazarus. The same word is used for the disciple 'whom the Lord loved'. What does this mean? The akashic records reveal this to us. Who was Lazarus after he had risen from the dead? He was none other than the writer of the Gospel of St. John, the Lazarus who was initiated by Christ. Christ poured into the soul of Lazarus the tidings of His own existence, so that the message of the fourth Gospel – the Gospel of St. John – might resound through the world as a description of Christ's own being.'

DO AS YOU DARN WELL PLEASEY

The Lambeth Walk is a walking dance that originated in the Limehouse district of London. Lambeth walkers strut along in a jaunty, confident manner, 'everything free and easy'. The dance was introduced into the US in the late 30s, where it merged with the old plantation Cakewalk and Swing to become the Champion Strut.

THE ULTIMATE FOOTWEAR CHECKLIST

Shoe-lovers everywhere, this is your chance to shine. Below are 40 types of footwear that you may once have owned. Perhaps you're wearing a pair of one of them right now? Tick the boxes to find out whether you're a pragmatist or a fetishist – and what shoes really mean to you.

☐ Platforms
☐ Winkle-pickers
☐ High heels
☐ Trainers
☐ Flats
☐ Mules
☐ Sandals
☐ Penny Loafers
☐ Ankle boots
☐ Pixie boots
☐ Snow boots
☐ Slip-ons
☐ Flip-flops
☐ Pumps
☐ Courts
☐ Knee-high boots
☐ Stilettos
☐ Louis XIV heel
☐ Wedges
☐ Moccasins

☐ Espadrilles
☐ Golf shoes
☐ Bowling shoes
☐ Toe thongs
☐ Oxfords
☐ Peep toes
☐ Hiking boots
☐ Cowboy boots
☐ Wellingtons
☐ Slingbacks
☐ Saddle shoes
☐ Riding boots
☐ Clogs
☐ Bovver boots
☐ Cycling shoes
☐ Army boots
☐ Slippers
☐ Ballet shoes
☐ Spats
☐ Tap shoes

Five pairs or fewer: Ah, never mind. You probably have the view that shoes are just there to get you from A to B. Bet two of those you ticked were hiking boots and slippers. And bet you've got odd socks on right now.

Six to 20 pairs: Experimentation has sometimes been your thing, but probably mainly in your youth, when you lasted three lessons of tap, and dressed like Bon Jovi the rest of the time. Bet boots of various styles figured highly on your list.

21 to 39 pairs: Ah, now here's someone with an understanding of feet. It's not about practicality, nor is it just about style. You shop at Shoes R Us, you take photographs of your collection, and your knee-highs aren't kept on the same shelf as your moccasins. Bet it's the clogs that are missing from your wardrobe, though.

All 40 pairs: Imelda, where have you been!

...only to be thrown out by the bouncer for not wearing a tie. He goes back to his car to move on, then is struck by an idea. Pulling out his jump leads, he ties them around his neck, and goes back into the bar again. 'There you go,' he grins. 'You didn't say what type of tie.' 'Alright, you can come in,' says the bouncer. 'But don't start anything.'

HORSE PLAY

Horses have four natural walking styles.

The walk

This is the slowest gait, in which the horse always has two or three hooves on the ground. The order in which it lifts its feet is:

Right hind
Right fore
Left hind
Left fore

The trot

Trotting is a simple two-step movement, in which the horse moves its legs from one diagonal to another. During each spring, all four legs are off the ground. The order in which it lifts its feet is:

Right fore/left hind
Left fore/right hind

The canter

This is a 3-beat movement, which results in a rocking motion. The order in which a right-sided horse lifts its feet is:

Left hind leg
Right hind/left fore
Right fore

The gallop

This is a similar movement to the canter, except that the horse's legs move one at a time. The order in which a right-sided horse lifts its feet is:

Left hind
Right hind
Left fore
Right fore

THE AGE FACTOR

A recent survey of comparative walking speeds between older and younger pedestrians crossing the road threw up the following results:
• The average walking speed for older pedestrians is 4.11 feet per second, compared with 4.95 for younger pedestrians.
• Older females have the slowest walking speed at 3.89 feet per second.
• The difference in speed between older men and older women is 0.42 feet per second; the difference between younger men and younger women is 0.32.

THE 5 MOST DANGEROUS ANIMALS
YOU'RE LIKELY TO ENCOUNTER WHILE
ON A WALKING SAFARI

Lion

Stand absolutely still and avoid eye contact. If it is during the day, the lion is likely to be too full to be interested in you.

Hippo

Make sure you do not get between the hippo and its water. If you do, run away from the water.

Buffalo

If it charges, run away very fast and hide behind a tree.

Elephant

If it charges, run away very fast and climb a tree.

Aardvark

Probably the most dangerous animal of all, as you are likely to trip up in one of its holes when you're running away from everything else.

WALK LIKE A TRIPOD

Williamson County, Texas, was named in 1848 after Judge Williamson, to whom 'nature had indeed been lavish of her mental gifts, but as if repenting of her prodigality in that line, she later afflicted him with a grievous physical burden; his right leg being drawn up at a right angle at the knee, necessitating the substitution of a wooden leg, which circumstances gave rise to the name by which he was familiarly known: Three-Legged-Willie'.

The three-legged symbol of the Isle of Man, or triskelion, is one of the oldest symbols known. It has appeared in Italian rock carvings, Greek vases from the 8th century BC, and was a symbol of great power in Norse and Sicilian cultures. The Manx version probably comes from Scandinavia, where it symbolised the movement of the sun through the heavens.

Three-legged versions are among the simpler and most often used robot designs, because their tripedal base gives them the stability that a two-legged robot can rarely acquire. R2-D2, the least irritating of the two Star Wars robots – or droids – demonstrated this mobility reasonably well, despite having an actor inside him.

Jake the Peg was not actually a three-legged man, just Rolf Harris mucking about with an artificial limb.

THE ULTIMATE CRICKET MATCH

It was the year 2135, and to celebrate the bicentenary of the Ramblers' Association, a match was arranged in heaven (which is where all cricketers go), between the Walkers' XI and the Wanderers' XI. The players were picked from various squads of 19th and 20th century England. After playing for nearly seven months, the match ended in a draw, four blisters and one bad case of athlete's foot.

THE WALKERS' XI	THE WANDERERS' XI
Walker, A	Ambler, J
(Northants and Durham, 1983-1987)	*(Somerset and Yorkshire, 1883-1886)*
Walker, AH	Boot, J
(Middlesex, 1855-1862)	*(Derbyshire, 1895)*
Walker, CW	Foot, AJ
(Gentlemen of the North, 1870)	*(Dorset, 1989)*
Walker, GG	Hele, AK
(Derbyshire, 1881-1898)	*(Devon, 1998-2001)*
Walker, ID	Hill, Lord AE
(Middlesex, 1862-1884)	*(MCC, 1841-1843)*
Walker, KDM	Payne, RBTS
(Cambridge University, 1999)	*(Somerset, 1906)*
Walker, KGE	Steptoe, GR
(DR Jardine's XI, 1955-1957)	*(Buckinghamshire squad member)*
Walker, LNP	Stride, KH
(Nottinghamshire, 1994-1997)	*(Staffordshire, Minor Counties, 1975-1978)*
Walker, NAD	Traill, GB
(Europeans and Derbyshire, 1923-1936)	*(MCC, 1864)*
Walker, PM	Trott, AE
(Glamorgan and England, 1956-1972)	*(Middlesex, England AND Australia, 1892-1910)*
Walker, SG	Trotter, DN
(Derbyshire, 1932)	*(North of England, 1877)*

The two 12th men were:
Came, KC *(Free Foresters, 1957)* and Went, GJH *(Glamorgan, 1934)*

WALK LIKE AN ANIMAL

Geckos are five-toed lizards that are common sights on walls and ceilings in tropical countries. Each foot is tipped with about 500,000 microscopic foot-hairs, each no more than about 5 microns in diameter, or about one-tenth the thickness of a human hair. The foot-hairs have split ends – too small to see without a microscope – that bond, rather like Velcro, with the surface upon which it walks.

RAMBLING RIDDLE

Unravel the following:

Walk   **It**

Answer on page 153.

10 BEAUTIFUL PICTURES FOR THE
STAY-AT-HOME WALKER

The Walk to Work	Jean Millet	1851
The Walkers	Claude Monet	1865
Cliff Walk at Pourville	Claude Monet	1882
The Walk in the Forest	Henri Rousseau	1886
A Morning Walk. Mrs Violet Ormond, Artist's Sister	John Singer Sargent	1888
The Walk (or Falling Leaves)	Vincent Van Gogh	1889
Landscape with Couple Walking and Crescent Moon	Vincent Van Gogh	1890
Sunlight Walk	Auguste Macke	1913
The Promenade	Marc Chagall	1918
Tightrope walker	Paul Klee	1923

QUOTE UNQUOTE

I was walking down the street wearing glasses when the prescription ran out.
STEVEN WRIGHT, comedian

LEFT, RIGHT, LEFT, RIGHT

• Between August 24, 1846, and January 21, 1847, the Mormon Battalion made one of the longest marches in US history • 2,000 miles between Missouri and California • to help secure California for the US.
• Napoleon's attempt to conquer Russia in 1812 ended in stunning defeat. Having left with nearly half a million soldiers, he made his march upon Moscow, yet found himself cut off from his supply lines, with the retreating Russians destroying each village and town behind them, including Moscow, to further decrease his supplies. Realising his mistake, and in the grip of a terrible winter, Napoleon turned for home, arriving back with barely 10,000 men.

QUOTE UNQUOTE

Of all exercises, walking is the best.
THOMAS JEFFERSON, US President

EDMUND HILLARY'S LOST BOOT

How did one right boot made for Edmund Hillary's expedition to conquer Mount Everest manage to survive untouched? That is a question often asked when people see this very heavy, hob-nailed, hand sewn brown boot which stands in a display of other boots and shoes at James Taylor & Son's shoe shop near Baker Street, London. Edmund Hillary ordered a pair of boots to be made for his expedition from Robert Laurie whose mountaineering workshops kitted out many explorers and mountaineers until they closed in 1980. The boots were posted to Hillary, whereby one was lost from the package on its way, so another boot was made for him. The missing boot was later recovered from the Post Office after Hillary reached the summit. It weighs over two pounds and has a double sewn sole holding the mid-sole to the upper to make it immensely strong and the sole is completely rigid so he could use it for climbing on small crevices and ledges.

5 AD SLOGANS

I'd walk a mile for a Camel ....Camel cigarettes

Let your fingers do the walking ....Yellow Pages

You walk a little taller in Levi's ....Levi's Jeans

Keep walking...Johnnie Walker Whisky

Lipsmackin'thirstquenchin'acetastin'
motivatin'goodbuzzin'cooltalkin'
highwalkin'fastlivin'evergivin'coolfizzin' ....Pepsi

WATER WALKS

MUDWALKS ON THE WADDEN SEA, THE NETHERLANDS

Covering 8,000km of Denmark, Germany and the Netherlands, the Wadden Sea is one of the largest tidal mudflats in the world. The region is inhabited by thousands of birds, innumerable marine crustaceans and molluscs and several species of marine mammals. Each year, 45,000 'mudwalkers' trek waist-deep in the sea's cold ooze. Mudwalking, or 'wadlopen' as the Dutch call it, occurs nowhere else on the planet.

Mudwalks range in difficulty from beginners' to advanced, and last between four and eight hours. A walk should only be attempted with a professional guide. Walkers must be physically fit, and between the ages of 12 and 65.

Patrick Leigh Fermor takes stock during a Carpathian upland walk.
I feared I might have got rusty, but all was well and my kit seemed in as good repair as the first day in Holland. The ammunition boots from Millets in the Strand, crunching along on their only slightly blunted hobnails, were still good for unlimited miles. The old breeches were soft with much wear and cleaning, and every stitch was intact; only the grey puttees had suffered minor damage, but nothing showed when I had snipped off the ragged edges where snow and rain had frayed them. A grey shirt with the sleeves rolled up completed this marching gear.

I blessed my stars that my first rucksack, with its complex framework and straps, heavy water-proof sleeping-bag and White Knight superfluity of gear had been stolen in Munich; the one my Baltic Russian friends had bestowed was smaller but held all I needed; to wit: a pair of dark flannel bags and another light canvas pair; a thick, decent-looking tweed jacket; several shirts; two ties, gym-shoes, lots of socks and jerseys, pyjamas, the length of coloured braid Angela had given me; a dozen new handkerchiefs and a sponge-bag, a compass, a jack-knife, two candles, matches, a pipe – falling into disuse – tobacco, cigarettes and – a new accomplishment – papers for rolling them, and a flask-filled in turn, as the countries changed, with whisky, Bols, schnapps, barack, tzuica, slivovitz, arak and tziporo. In one of the side pockets there was a five-shilling Ingersoll watch that kept perfect time when I remembered to take it out and wind it up.

The only awkward item was the soldier's greatcoat; I hadn't worn it for months, but felt reluctant to get rid of it. I still had the Hungarian walking-stick, intricately carved as a mediaeval crosier, the second replacement for the original ninepenny ashplant from the tobacconist's off Sloane Square. Apart from sketch-book, pencils and disintegrating maps, there was my notebook-journal and my passport. (Dog-eared and faded, these sole survivors are both within reach at this moment.) There was Hungarian and Rumanian Self-Taught (little progress in the one, hesitant first steps in the other); I was re-reading Antic Hay; and there was Schlegel & Tieck's Hamlet, Prinz von Danemark, bought in Cologne; also, given by the same kind hand as the rucksack, and carefully wrapped up, the beautiful little seventeenth-century duodecimo Horace from Amsterdam. It was bound in stiff, grass-green leather; the text had long s's; mezzotint vignettes of Tibur, Lucretilis and Bandusian spring, a scarlet silk marker, the giver's bookplate and a skeleton-leaf from his Estonian woods.

It would have been hard to set off much later than the cock crew that morning as the bird itself was flapping its wings on a barrel ten yards away, so I sloshed some water on my face and set off. It was going to be a sizzling day.

Between the Woods and the Water, Patrick Leigh Fermor

You might not find marathons mentioned elsewhere in this volume, since the 26 miles of such races are generally covered by runners rather than walkers. But one participant in the 2002 London Marathon 'ran' it in a time of five days, eight hours, 29 minutes and 46 seconds. Lloyd Scott, from Rainham in Essex thereby became its slowest ever participant – and finished much more slowly than most ramblers would. This feat of snail-like perambulation was achieved thanks to the kit chosen by the athlete. Mr. Scott decided to forgo the lightweight shorts and vest worn by most entrants and instead went for a 120lb 1940s diving suit. Despite these efforts, the Guinness Book of Records has refused to grant the title of 'world's slowest marathon runner' to the 40-year-old former fireman and professional footballer since the race is designed to be a fast event. Scott's travails eventually earned more than £100,000 for Bristol-based charity Cancer and Leukaemia in Childhood (Clic), a cause close to his heart since he had previously suffered from the disease. Seven months later, he ran the New York marathon on behalf of the families of firemen killed in the September 11th attacks, this time managing to shave an incredible eight hours off his previous time.

RAMBLING RIDDLE

Unravel the following. Answer on page 153.
STEP PETS PETS

6 TIPS WHEN BUYING BOOTS

Beware of high street fashion boots that look like walking boots. They may not give the protection you need.

Feet expand during the day so go shopping in the afternoon.

Try to visit a shop with an incline board so you can test boots for your downward foot position. If unavailable, put your heel on a step and your toe to the floor. If your foot slips forward it isn't the right boot.

If you can't find perfectly fitting boots, ask the shop assistant for footbeds or insoles.

Take a pair of your usual walking socks with you when going to buy boots. The thickness makes a huge difference to the fit.

Don't buy boots second-hand. A worn-in pair of boots has been shaped to suit the previous owner's feet and walking style, so probably won't suit yours.

OPEN GAITS

Whether you stroll, lurch or lumber, scientists are studying ways to identify and track you by the way you walk. Just as people are recognised by their facial features or patterns of speech, scientists are researching methods of 'Gait Recognition'. All of the above comes under the broad title of 'Biometrics' – the science of identifying people through physiological or behavioural characteristics.

Physical differences in, for example, the width or orientation of the pelvis, mean that everyone walks in a distinctive way. Computer-based statistical models are now being used to do what people do instinctively - that is either recognising the figure walking ahead as being familiar, or as a complete stranger. Researchers at the Georgia Institute of Technology, Atlanta are teaching computers to record the precise way that people move. Volunteers wearing metallic discs walk through a studio, while the computers monitor the position of each disc and build up a digital picture of the person's gait. The computers are then able to recognise the volunteers when they walk past in a different location to the one in which they were recorded. Gait-recognition technology has great potential in aiding security services in the future. Significant refinements do need to be made, as the computer sensors are at present unable to pick out one person from other background movements such as a busy street.

WALKING WORDS

I cannot see the wit of walking and talking at the same time. When I am in the country, I wish to vegetate like the country. I am not for criticising hedge-rows and black cattle. I go out of town in order to forget the town and all that is in it. There are those who for this purpose go to watering-places, and carry the metropolis with them. I like more elbow-room, and fewer incumbrances. I like solitude, when I give myself up to it, for the sake of solitude.

On Going a Journey, William Hazlitt, essayist

WATER WALKS

LIHOU ISLAND, GUERNSEY
Lihou Island, off Guernsey, is linked to the mainland only by a tidal causeway. From Vazon Bay, take the road West to Perelle Bay and continue towards Fort Saumarez. Turn right up the lane and cross the car park towards the island. By the shore a notice gives causeway-crossing times. On Lihou is the ruined Priory of St. Mary, affiliated to Mont Saint Michel Abbey off mainland France.

What are shake holes?
These are steep-sided holes, or funnel-shaped dips in the ground that appear on some OS maps since they are considered hazardous. Often found in areas where porous limestone forms the base rock, they occur when soil at the surface is drawn into holes underground.

What's the difference between a hamlet, a village and a town?
A hamlet is usually defined as a small, isolated group of houses without a church. A village, on the other hand, must always have a church but has an area of less than one square mile. A town is a centre both of population and business with an area greater than 2.5 square kilometres, although smaller communities are sometimes traditionally described as towns (as in the case of market towns or county towns).

What's the difference between hills and mountains?
There is no international classification of mountains, and the Ordnance Survey does not use one, but in its literature tries to adhere to local nomenclature. In England, Wales and Ireland, the minimum height is generally agreed to be 2000 feet.

But two further views hold that every summit above this height should be designated a mountain, or that a mountain should have a distinct summit or peak.

According to the first classification, therefore, Kinder Scout (636m) in the Peak District National Park would be defined as a mountain. According to the second school of thought, it should be considered as high moorland since it has no obvious summit. A further qualification might well be needed: a mountain must lie north of 51 degrees in order to account for Yes Tor and High Willhays on Dartmoor. They are both higher than 2000 feet and have peaks, but are never classified as mountains.

Where is the emptiest square on an OS map?
In fact, there are no completely empty squares on 1:25,000 or 1:50,000-scale Ordnance Survey maps of Great Britain. The grid scale with the least amount of detail is at SE 8322 on OS Landranger map 112 (Scarborough and Gainsborough sheet). The only feature in the field that appears in this square is the line of a pylon.

Where is the furthest point in Great Britain from a metalled road?
The A832 is 11km, or seven miles, away from the hillside of Ruadh Stac Beag between Letterwe Forest and Fisherfield Forest in Wester Ross, Highland, Scotland (NH 025770).

HOW DOES A COMPASS WORK?

No matter where you stand on earth, if you hold a compass in your hand it will point to the magnetic north pole. How come? The compass is in fact an extremely simple device, consisting of a small, lightweight magnet (the needle) which is balanced on a nearly frictionless pivot point. The needle always aligns itself with the Earth's magnetic field, which is created by electrical currents in the slowly moving molten iron of the earth's outer core. This magnetic field runs on a North-South orientation, so the compass always points north.

QUOTE UNQUOTE

If man walks in the woods for love of them half of each day, he is in danger of being regarded as a loafer; but if he spends his whole day as a speculator, shearing off those woods and making earth bald before her time, he is esteemed as an industrious and enterprising citizen.
HENRY DAVID THOREAU, US writer and naturalist

HALF PACE

Number of paces recommended per day by the US Surgeon General:
10,000
Number of paces taken each day by the average American:
5,000

10 FAMOUS LITERARY WALKERS

Jean-Jacques Rousseau (1712-78), French writer and philosopher

Thomas Jefferson (1743-1826) Third American president

William Wordsworth (1770-1850) English Poet Laureate

Samuel Taylor Coleridge (1772-1834) English poet and philosopher

Thomas de Quincey (1785-1859) English critic and essayist

Charles Dickens (1812-70) English novelist

Henry David Thoreau (1812-62) American naturalist and writer

Walt Whitman (1818-92) American poet and revered father figure

John Ruskin (1819-1900) English author and critic

George Macaulay Trevelyan (1876-1962) English historian

The Ramblers

ENJOY THE COUNTRYSIDE

'Love it', laughed Bob to himself as the gulls topped up Gill's drink

WALK LIKE AN ANIMAL

'They look like catfish but can obviously survive for long periods out of water. They propel themselves by their fins on land, even climbing uphill.'

This was how the journal *Scientific American* described the introduction of the 'suffering catfish', genus Clarius, into Florida lakes in 1969. A later story records an aggressive and voracious fish attacking a dog in a park that was nowhere near water. The catfish are natives of South Asia and Africa. Air chambers extending up into the skull, each occupied by a 'respiratory tree' that is richly vascularized for the exchange of oxygen and carbon dioxide between the air and the fish's blood enables the fish to stay out of water for 12 hours or more.

CROSS WORDS

Zebra crossing	Named after black and white stripes.
Pelican crossing	Abbreviation of PEdestrian LIght CONtrol (so its actually 'Pelicon').
Puffin crossing	Rough abbreviation of Pedestrian User Friendly INtelligent crossing (the green man is situated above the button, and detectors can extend the time available for pedestrians to cross the road).
Toucan crossing	For cyclists and pedestrians – often linked to a cycleway – hence 'two can' cross.
Pegasus crossing	Traffic-light controlled crossing point that caters for pedestrians, cyclists and horse riders. The horse riders have a separate waiting area, which incorporates a high-level push button that they can operate without dismounting.

QUOTE UNQUOTE

Don't walk behind me, I may not lead. Don't walk in front of me; I may not follow. Just walk beside me and be my friend.
ALBERT CAMUS, philosopher

POTENTIAL RAMBLING ANTHEMS

Walking With Thee – Clinic

Walking By Myself
Gary Moore

Walk Away
Sisters Of Mercy

Just Keep Walking – INXS

Walking In The Park With Eloise
The Country Hams

Walking With Mr Wheeze
Madness

Walking In The Rain
Grace Jones

Walking In The Sand
Shangri-Las

Walk A Thin Line
Fleetwood Mac

Walking Through The Ruins
Spilt Enz

THE RULES OF WALKABOUT

The Australian Aboriginal concept of 'walkabout' promotes self-discovery and challenge as important parts of our life's passage. Yet, traditionally, walkabouts are completed in pairs, discussing an issue or dilemma with a partner.

There are certain accepted rules acknowledged by two people who go walkabout together.

1. The conversation is confidential, and may not be repeated to anyone else. Similarly, neither partner may later approach the other for an update on the conversation, unless previously agreed.

2. Each partner has the same amount of time to discuss their issues.

3. The pace should never be hurried. The third occasional partner on a walkabout is silence.

RAMBLING RIDDLE

If the population of China walked past you in single file, the line would never end. Why?
Answer on page 153.

QUOTE UNQUOTE

I only went out for a walk and finally concluded to stay out till sundown, for going out, I found, was really going in.
JOHN MUIR,
naturalist and writer

FOOT CARE – THE 5 EASY STEPS TO SKIN PROTECTION

1. Use your own foot protection and shoes. Don't share shoes or socks.
2. Buy the best socks – a cotton/acrylic mix. Cotton absorbs moisture, but holds it close to the skin.
3. Keep your feet as dry as possible. Use foot powders if your feet sweat a lot.
4. Avoid wearing shoes of man-made materials, like plastic and vinyl, for long periods of time.
5. Give your feet breathing time. Go barefoot as often as possible, although be careful at public pools or spas.

THE WANDERING MINSTRELS

The family made famous by the 1965 Hollywood musical starring Julie Andrews was based on a true story. Captain Von Trapp did indeed marry a former nun who joined the family of seven children. They had three further children of their own and the final family of 12 formed the Von Trapp family singers. However, once Nazi Germany annexed Austria in 1938 they decided to flee their native country.

The Hollywood movie depicted the family fleeing the Nazis after a concert, walking over the Alps to freedom in Switzerland. In real life the family crossed the Alps to Italy. Once they had escaped the Third Reich on foot, they travelled to the US and settled in Stowe, Vermont where they continued to sing as a family to earn money.

QUOTE UNQUOTE

Thoughts come clearly while one walks.
THOMAS MANN, novelist

AND MILES TO GO BEFORE I SLEEP

Milestones are almost obsolete today, except as a historical record. Modern transport does not require milestones, which are practically invisible to motorists. However, for several centuries milestones were the only form of reference for walkers before maps had been standardised. They not only let walkers know where they were but they were also used to time mailcoaches and walking races and work out the cost of postage and of hiring horses.

The Romans first defined the centre of Imperial Rome with the 'Golden Milestone' and placed milestones on their roads showing the distance to this datum so travellers could mark their progress. The Millarium Aureum was the first golden milestone and was erected by the Emperor Augustus in 20 BC. This milestone marked the point from which the major imperial highways radiated.

In more remote parts of Britain such as the Peak District and the Yorkshire Moors, travellers often perished as they became lost without features to orient themselves. In an attempt to do something about this needless loss of life, William III decreed that guide stones be erected in such regions in 1697.

Since the advent of the car, milestones have become less relevant but in recent years their importance as historical landmarks has been recognised and they are now being preserved and restored.

THE MAGIC ROPE TRICK

Tightrope walking is also known as funambulism – from the Latin funis (rope) and ambulare (walk). Wire walking, although similar, is the art of walking a distance on an elevated wire that's approximately 1/2 inch thick. Sometimes, the wire walker holds a long pole, up to 12 metres in length to help balance.

The roots of the high wire's roots are as old as ancient Egypt and first century China, where the art of 'rope dancing' was performed over knives.

In the 1850s, Jean Francois Gravelet alias Charles Blondin (1824–1897) of France, received world acclaim for cooking and eating an omelette (complete with stove and neatly set table) on a high wire stretched over Niagara Falls.

In 1887 tightrope walker Steven Peer fell to his death while performing a stunt over Niagara Falls

The Niagara Parks Commission now prohibits stunting on all of its properties under the authority granted by the Regulations of the Niagara Parks Act. Stunting now carries a maximum fine of $10,000.

Acrobat Ahdili tightrope-walked on a wire 35 metres above the ground for 22 days to break the Guinness World Record. During this time, the acrobat covered a distance of 200 kilometres, wearing out three pairs of boots.

10 SURE SIGNS YOU'RE A WALKING NUT

1. You have seven pairs of knee-length woollen socks of which two come in sunset red.
2. You can prepare a cheese and tomato sandwich with just one hand.
3. You wear a bobble hat, but only as a post-modern statement.
4. You tie plastic bags around your boots when you enter a pub.
5. You swap blister stories like an army veteran.
6. You don't just know that dock cures nettle stings, you actually know what dock looks like.
7. You can tell the difference between a chiffchaff and a willow warbler without even hearing them sing.
8. You paper your walls with old OS maps.
9. You once considered buying mini windscreen wipers for your glasses.
10. You know you're obsessed, but as walking is truly the greatest pleasure on this earth, then so what.

HOW TO WALK UP A SLOPE

If there are two of you, lean against each other to tackle the incline. This position lessens the weight on your legs and makes the climb easier – although outbursts of laughter can often counteract the benefits.

FOOT AND MOUTH DISEASE

Foot and mouth disease (FMD) is an acute infectious viral disease causing fever, followed by the development of vesticles (blisters) chiefly in the mouth and on the feet. It is probably more infectious than any other disease affecting animals and spreads rapidly if uncontrolled. It affects cattle, sheep, pigs, goats. Wild and domestic cloven hooved animals are susceptible, as are hedgehogs and rats.

Clinical signs to look for in cattle
Slobbering and smacking lips
Shivering
Tender and sore feet
Reduced milk yield
Sores and blisters on feet
Raised temperature

The British Tourist Authority (BTA) estimates that the outbreak of FMD in 2001 helped drive tourism down by about 10% from the previous year, resulting in an estimated loss of £41 million.

9 FICTIONAL CHARACTERS WHO COULD SO EASILY HAVE BEEN WALKERS

Rambleotiltskin	Ramblo	Trekkie Mr Sock
Harry Trotter	Mr Picknick	A fish called Wander
Walker Mitty	Willy Walka	...and Luke Skywalker

A MAN WALKS INTO A BAR...

...and says 'Got any grapes?' The barman says: 'Grapes? Course I haven't got any grapes. This is a pub.'
The man leaves, but is back the next night. 'Got any grapes?'
'Look,' says the barman, 'I already told you I don't have any grapes. You ask me that one more time, I'll nail your head to the bar.'
The man leaves again, but sure enough he's there the following night. 'Got any nails?'
The barman looks puzzled. 'No.'
'Good. Got any grapes?'

THESE BOOTS ARE MADE
FOR MOTORISED WALKING

An inventor has produced a pair of walking boots with tiny combustion engines which are set for production in Russia. Viktor Gordejcv, from the Ural Mountains, drew inspiration from his time in the Soviet army when he wished he had engines on his boots to help finish military marches.

The boots use the tiny engines in each foot so that as soon as the wearer steps forward with one foot, the engines propel the other one forward. The boots, which will be 'launched' in Russia, will retail for about £600 a pair.

WALKING WORDS

At three o'clock Cummings and Gowing called for a good long walk over Hampstead and Finchley, and brought with them a friend named Stillbrook. We walked and chatted together, except Stillbrook, who was always a few yards behind us staring at the ground and cutting at the grass with his stick.

As it was getting on for five, we four held a consultation, and Gowing suggested that we should make for The Cow and Hedge and get some tea. Stillbrook said a brandy and soda was good enough for him. I reminded them that all public houses were closed till six o'clock. Stillbrook said, 'That's alright – bona-fide travellers.'

We arrived; and as I was trying to pass, the man in charge of the gate said: 'Where from?' I replied: 'Holloway'. He immediately put up his arm, and declined to let me pass. I turned back for a moment, when I saw Stillbrook, closely followed by Cummings and Gowing, make for the entrance. I watched them, and thought I would have a good laugh at their expense. I heard the porter say: 'Where from?' When, to my surprise, in fact disgust, Stillbrook replied: 'Blackheath,' and the three were immediately admitted.

Gowing called to me across the gate, and said: 'We shan't be a minute.' I waited for them the best part of an hour.

The Diary of a Nobody,
George and Weedon Grossmith

WHAT HAVE THE RAMBLERS EVER DONE FOR US?

The Ramblers' Association works to increase walking opportunities for all in both town or country. This work would not be possible without the financial and practical support of volunteers and members.

ANIMALS THAT USE THEIR LEGS OTHER THAN FOR WALKING

Kangaroos move by hopping on their hind legs at speeds up to 40mph/60kmh, using their tail for steering and balancing. When the kangaroo is moving slowly the tail is used as an extra leg to support the animal.

Most kangaroos can only move both back legs together and not one at a time.

Grasshoppers 'sing' by rubbing their hind legs against their forewings. One of these has pegs on it, the other a hard ridge, giving off a sound similar to that of a distant stringed instrument. It is mainly the courting males that we hear giving off their songs, although in some species the female also has a quiet answering song.

Moles have stubby, broad, shovel-like front feet, which are extremely well adapted for digging.

Crustaceans have ten legs that perform specialised tasks. Their three middle legs are for walking sideways on the seabed, and their front pair, the strong pincer claws, for defence and predation. The remaining pair, the hind legs that resemble paddles, enable the animal to swim, hence the crab's Latin name, Callinectes or 'beautiful swimmer'.

QUOTE UNQUOTE

And the Lord saith unto Satan, Whence comest thou? Then Satan answered the Lord, and said, From going to and fro in the earth, and from walking up and down in it.
THE BOOK OF JOB

A MAN WALKS INTO A BAR...

...and orders a drink. The bartender gives him his drink, along with a bowl of peanuts. As the man dips in for a nut, a voice comes from the peanut bowl. 'Wow, you look fabulous tonight!' it says. 'Great hair, great aftershave... a class act all the way!'
The man is a little confused, so he gets up to get some cigarettes from the machine. He puts in his money, and another voice says: 'Hey, dorkhead. You gonna foul up the air around me any longer? Shoulda stayed at home, you should, with a face like that.'
The man reels backwards, and asks the barman what on earth is going on. 'Didn't you see the signs, sir? The peanuts are complimentary, but the cigarette machine is out of order.'

Unravel the following:
WALK
DIES
Answer on page 153.

WALKING SIDE BY SIDE

Improve your vocabulary, with the words in the Oxford English Reference Dictionary that are immediately before and after walking words.

Ambivert – a person who fluctuates between being an introvert and an extrovert.	AMBLE	**Amblyopia** – dimness of vision without obvious defect or change in the eye.
Hijra – variant of Hegira, Muhammad's departure from Mecca to Medina in AD622, which marks the consolidation of the first Muslim community.	HIKE	**Hila** – plural of Hilum, the point of attachment of a seed to its seed-vessel.
Rambert – Dame Marie (1888-1982), British ballet-dancer, teacher, and director, born in Poland.	RAMBLE RAMBLER RAMBLING	**Rambo** – the hero of David Morrell's novel First Blood (1972), a Vietnam War veteran characterized as macho, self-sufficient, and bent on violent retribution.
Strike – the act or an instance of striking; a blow or hit	STROLL STROLLER	**Stroma** – the framework of an organ or cell, or a fungous tissue containing spore-producing bodies.
Trahison des clercs – the betrayal of standards, scholarship, etc, by intellectuals.	TRAIL	**Trailer** – a vehicle towed by another, or a series of brief extracts from a film used to advertise it in advance.
Walian – a native or inhabitant of (a specified region of) Wales.	WALK	**Walkabout** – an informal stroll among a crowd by a visiting dignitary, or a period of wandering in the bush by an Australian Aboriginal.

WALK LIKE AN ANIMAL

The dipper is a British water bird shaped like a large wren, that has a unique way of hunting its prey. It feeds on water snails and the larvae of caddis flies, which it grabs from below the surface of fast-running waters by walking along the bed of the stream, completely submerged. It walks into the current, its strong claws gripping the bottom, while it flicks pebbles with its beak looking for food. Using the flow of the current to help press it down, the dipper can remain underwater for up to 23 seconds.

JUST POPPING OUT TO POST A LETTER

In 1997, social psychologist Robert Levine published the results of his lengthy survey into the comparative paces of life of the inhabitants of 31 countries. One of the parameters he used to draw his conclusions was 'the number of minutes downtown pedestrians take to walk 60 feet' – (the others were 'minutes it takes a postal clerk to complete a stamp-purchase transaction', and 'accuracy in minutes of public clocks').

The ranking of the 31 countries for the walking bit was as follows, with Ireland being the fastest:

1 Ireland	9 Kenya	17 Mexico	24 China
2 Netherlands	10 Italy	18 Taiwan	25 Singapore
3 Switzerland	11 Canada	19 Hungary	26 Indonesia
4 England	12 Poland	20 South Korea	27 Bulgaria
5 Germany	13 Sweden	21 Czech	28 Jordan
6 United States	=14 Hong	Republic	29 Syria
7 Japan	Kong/Greece	22 El Salvador	30 Romania
8 France	16 Costa Rica	23 Austria	31 Brazil

A MAN WALKS INTO A BAR...

...and settles down with his drink next to a little fellow who's staring miserably at his scotch. After about 20 minutes, the little guy is still just sitting there, so the first man grabs the scotch and drinks it down. The little chap starts to cry.

'Hey, I'm sorry,' says the first man, 'but I thought maybe you didn't want it. Let me buy you another.'

'No, it's not that. This day is the worst of my life. First, I oversleep, get to work late, and my boss fires me. When I leave the building to go to my car, I find it's stolen. I get a cab home, but leave my wallet in it. I get inside my front door, and find my wife in bed with my brother.

'Then to top it all off, I come to this bar, and just as I'm thinking of finishing it all, you show up and drink my poison.'

HOW TO RECOGNISE TREES WITHOUT RESORTING TO ILLUSTRATIONS

Name	Bark	Leaves	Trunks/ Branches	Extras
Ash	Pale grey and covered with irregular dents running downwards	Occur in pairs of 4 or 6 opposite one another on the stalk	Branches curve and droop slightly	Can be up to 100 feet
Beech	Smooth and grey	Oval, running to a sharp point at the top	Often grows to 60 feet before starting to branch out	Lives to great age Can reach 100 feet
Horse Chestnut	Grey and smooth, but when older carries deep undulations	Large leaves with 5 to 7 leaflets, with narrow base and oval top	Branches grow up-wards but in compact and orderly way	Height span of 60-70 feet Life span of 150-200 years
Elm	Slippery elm bark is used in medication	Oval and running to a well defined point	There are usually one or two very large branches	Can reach 120 feet Circumference can reach 20 feet
Yew	Thin reddish brown bark which peels off easily	Narrow and pointed, about an inch long	Branches grow up from the base, joining with the trunk	In middle ages it provided bows for bowmen Height ranges from 20-50 feet
Scots Pine	Brown – purple in colour, coarsely fissured	Leaves are bluish green and grow from the stem in pairs	Branches form at intervals and bend down toward ends	Can reach 100 feet
Sycamore	Bark is smooth and veined.	The leaves are blue-green on the underside and have 5 lobes	Lower branches horizontal, upper angle at 45 degrees	Grows to maximum of 60 feet

WALKING AND BRAS

According to walking writer Wendy Bumgardner the seven problems of walking in a normal bra are:

Strap attack • Staying hooked
Moisture Control • Appearance
Motion control without compression
Chafing • Support

WALKING WORDS

He and my father would often go for walks along the Warsaw Highway which cut across the countryside not far from our house. Sometimes I accompanied them. Scriabin liked to take a run and then to go on skipping along the road like a stone skimming the water, as if at any moment he might leave the ground and glide on air. In general, he had trained himself in various kinds of sublime lightness and unburdened movement verging on flight. Among such expressions of his character were his well-bred charm and his worldly manner of putting on a splendid air and avoiding serious subjects in society.

An essay in Autobiography, Boris Pasternak

QUOTE UNQUOTE

A first walk in any new country is one of the things which make life on this planet worth being grateful for.
CHARLES WILLIAM BEEBE,
US explorer and naturalist

10 TOP TIPS FOR WALKING WITH YOUR KIDS

1. Be enthusiastic – it can be contagious

2. Don't try to walk too far

3. Avoid strenuous routes

4. Set your pace to that of the slowest walker

5. Find a route which has points of interest for kids. Boredom can be their biggest enemy

6. Set easily-attainable objectives

7. Bring plenty of snacks and drinks

8. Stop often for rest or refreshment

9. Be prepared to stop your walk when children tire

10. Finally, always praise them at the end

RAIN WALKING

Alessandro De Angelis, a physicist at the University of Udine, Italy, calculated some years ago that a sprinter racing along at 22.4 miles an hour does get less wet, but only 10% less wet, than a fast stroller (6.7 miles an hour). However, further tests on two men who ran and walked a 100 metre course on a rainy day wearing identical sweat suits and hats, which they'd weighed before the test, resulted in the walker absorbing about seven and a half ounces, and the runner sopping up only four and a half, a 40% reduction in dampness. Nonetheless the message is clear: running through the rain really does keep you drier.

QUOTE UNQUOTE

Walking connects you to the land, it sews a seam between you and it that is very hard to unstitch.
KELLY WINTERS,
writer

RAMBLING RIDDLE

One word follows the first word below and precedes the second to make two new words. What is it?
WALK DRAKE
Answer on page 153.

WATER WALKS

ROUGH ISLAND, DUMFRIES

A National Trust for Scotland bird reserve, Rough Island lies off the coast of Dumfries opposite Rockcliffe. The shingle causeway to the island leads off the NTS Jubilee Path, an amenable round trip of 2 miles, taking 1 hour 15 minutes. The route takes in local landmarks such as the ruined Mote of Mark, while in summer beautiful plants flower in the meadows alongside.

WALK LIKE A STAR

Jack Lemmon and Tony Curtis were just two men among many who appreciated the Monroe wiggle. She achieved her trademark walk by cutting a quarter inch off one of her heels.

THE 12 STATIONS OF THE CROSS

The Stations, or Way of the Cross, are a traditional way of meditating on Christ's suffering and death, based on his final walk.

1. Jesus is condemned to death

2. Jesus receives the cross

3. Jesus falls for the first time

4. Jesus meets his blessed Mother

5. The cross is laid on Simon of Cyrene

6. Veronica wipes the face of Jesus

7. Jesus falls for the second time

8. Jesus meets the women of Jerusalem

9. Jesus falls for the third time

10. Jesus is stripped of his garments

11. Jesus is nailed to the cross

12. Jesus dies on the cross

MAD FOR WALKING

An anonymous American woman who set out on 1 January 1953, the 'Peace Pilgrim' vowed to 'remain a wanderer until mankind has learned the way of peace'. This remarkable character continued criss-crossing the USA for the subsequent 28 years, relying on strangers to shelter and feed her. Fate, in its inimitable cruelty, ended her travels when she was killed in a head-on car crash while being driven to a speaking engagement.

HOW TO PUT UP A MEMORIAL BENCH

Contact the local county council environmental services department. They will need to know:

Which bench would you like to purchase (local councils may specify a range of designs for you to choose from)

Inscription details and type of plaque

Where you wish the bench to be placed (often restricted to council-owned land).

Benches usually cost between £350 – £500. Make sure the bench is installed with tamper-proof fittings and check the agreement for long-term maintenance with the council. The whole process usually takes around three months.

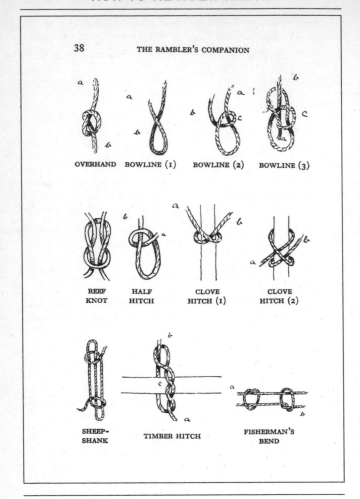

38   THE RAMBLER'S COMPANION

OVERHAND   BOWLINE (1)   BOWLINE (2)   BOWLINE (3)

REEF KNOT   HALF HITCH   CLOVE HITCH (1)   CLOVE HITCH (2)

SHEEPSHANK   TIMBER HITCH   FISHERMAN'S BEND

IF THE SHOE FITS

To find out if your walking shoes fit properly, trace the outline of your foot on a piece of paper and cut it out, suggests the American Academy of Orthopaedic Surgeons. If the paper cutout doesn't fit flat in the bottom of your shoe, it's time to find a more forgiving pair.

THE 13 UK NATIONAL PARKS
IN ORDER OF SIZE

1. Cairngorms
(1,400 sq miles)

2. Lake District (885)

3. Snowdonia (827)

4. Loch Lomond & the Trossachs
(720)

5. Yorkshire Dales
(683)

6. Peak District (555)

7. North York Moors
(554)

8. Brecon Beacons (519)

9. Northumberland (405)

10. Dartmoor (368)

11. Exmoor (268)

12. Pembrokeshire Coast
(240)

13. The Broads (117)

Two more parks, the New Forest
and the South Downs, are in the
pipeline for elevation to National
Park status.

QUOTE UNQUOTE

I walk regularly for my soul and my body tags along.
SARAH BAN BREATHNACH, writer

THE SHOE LADY

Probably the world's best known shoe collector is former Philippine First Lady Imelda Marcos, who amassed a collection of 1,220 pairs.

That's what was reportedly found once the personal quarters of the presidential palace was raided after the shoe fanatic and her husband had been chased from the country. Mrs. Marcos strongly refuted the claims and declared that she owned a mere 1,060 pairs. This was not a claim the people of the Philippines were particularly impressed by once they found out their first lady had been living in luxury while they starved, and that she and her husband stole an estimated 6 billion dollars when they were ousted after their regime fell in 1986. After 21 years in power the couple fled to Hawaii where Ferdinand died in 1989. Imelda lived on however and donated hundreds of pairs of shoes, all size eight and a half, to a museum she opened in 2001.

BLOCKED PASSAGES

There are a staggering 178,000 obstacles on the rights of way network in England and Wales – such as barbed wire, ploughing and cropping of paths, dangerous or missing stiles, gates, and signposts – making 31% of the paths in England and half of those in Wales difficult or impossible to use. Walkers can expect to come across an obstruction every 2km. It is up to local authorities to protect paths, and they currently need to invest £69.1 million to return the network to full working order.

6 LONDON STREETS FOR WALKERS

QUOTE UNQUOTE

The true charm of pedestrianism does not lie in the walking, or in the scenery, but in the talking. The walking is good to time the movement of the tongue by, and to keep the blood and the brain stirred up and active; the scenery and the woodsy smells are good to bear in upon a man an unconscious and unobtrusive charm and solace to eye and soul and sense; but the supreme pleasure comes from the talk.

MARK TWAIN, American writer

WHAT HAVE THE RAMBLERS EVER DONE FOR US?

It is the work done by the Ramblers' Association that is behind many of the long distance paths and national parks that are loved by walkers today.

WALK LIKE AN ANIMAL

Although a fish in water may not seem surprising, the Caribbean bottom-dwelling batfish has developed pectoral fins that resemble legs which it uses to propel itself along the sea floor. When folded, these legs look like bat wings, hence its name.

MODERN PILGRIMAGES

As a centre of pilgrimage, Glastonbury has different meanings for different people. For Christians Glastonbury is the revered site of the first Christian church built in the British Isles by Joseph of Arimathea. For others it is the resting place of Arthur and the home of the quest for the Grail and all the legends that surround it. Glastonbury is a worldwide recognised site of pilgrimage, not only for Christian pilgrims but pilgrims of every denomination and belief. The growing interest in sacred places has led to a modern awakening in the value of pilgrimage. In every age there have been pilgrims travelling to the sacred sites and places of the world as an act of spiritual devotion to their particular creed.

12 FILMS THAT WALKERS MIGHT WANT TO CATCH

The Dog Walker 2003

The Snow Walker 2003

Time Walker 1982

The Night Walker 1965

Johnnie Walker 1992

The Sleep Walker 1911

Wall Street Walker 1970

Dead Man Walking
1988, 1995

Should Sleepwalkers Marry?
1927

Pimple's the Case of Johnny Walker 1915

The Bibulous Wire Walker 1902

Walker
1987, 1992

EROTIC FEET

In September 1992 David Mellor was forced to resign as National Heritage secretary after his toe-sucking affair with actress Antonia de Sanchez was splashed across the tabloids.

QUOTE UNQUOTE

Walking is easiest, you don't need a lot of apparatus. Just shoe leather and good feet.
PAUL DUDLEY WHITE,
cardiologist

Number of miles walked by Centurion competitor 129
Geoff Tranter in 24 hours in 1981

The French have created some of the most efficient trails in Europe that cover over 110,000 miles and deliberately pass through what the French have every reason to take national pride in; their most sublime countryside. The Fédération Française de la Randonnée Pédestre (FFRP), known in English as the French Walking Federation established and still maintains the French trail system. The trails are organised into three specific types of path:

1. Sentiers de grande randonnée
Abbreviated to GR.
These are the long national paths which handily connect one point to another. They are numbered accordingly – GR 3, GR 60, etc. For example: the GR 5 runs from the Luxembourg border all the way down the Vosges, Jura and Alp mountains to the Mediterranean. There are approximately 38,000 miles of GR trails in France which are marked on the ground in white on red.

2. Regional paths
Abbreviated to GRPs.
These cover over 25,000 miles.

Each one covers a specific region, often in a circular layout that can be well over 100 miles long. They are marked on the ground in yellow on red.

3. Local paths
Abbreviated to PRs.
On maps, these paths are so numerous thay often intersect, forming a confused yellow blaze of colour. The start of these trails will most likely be found within urban areas, providing access to local beauty spots, areas of historical interest or simply can be used as a convenient way to experience rural France 'sans l'auto'. The paths range from an hour to a day's walk and are marked on the ground in yellow. There are 47,000 miles of documented local paths in France. In reality, this is a fraction of the total.

For a very detailed picture, these paths are best viewed on IGN 1:25,000 blue series published by The Institut Géographique National (IGN). 1:1,000,000 IGN map #903 is not detailed, but shows the whole trail system across France.
See www.ffrp.asso.fr.

WALKING AND BRAS

Bra burning is actually a myth. In 1968 American women marched in protest at the Miss America pageant. During the march they threw cosmetics, suspenders, high-heeled shoes and bras into a trash can to symbolise their freedom from male domination. Draft burning (burning draft papers) was a popular way of demonstrating against the US war in Vietnam and somehow the two got mixed.

WATER WALKS

BROUGH O' BIRSAY, ORKNEY

For centuries, political and religious power in Orkney was centred on the Brough o' Birsay, a small tidal island off the north-western corner of the Mainland. Inhabited variously by Christian missionaries, Picts and Norsemen since the fifth century AD, wildlife abounds on the Brough: puffins, auks and skuas can all be seen. The island can be reached on foot from the Bay of Skaill, a distance of around five and a half miles. From the bay, head North towards Birsay through the hills of Marwick. Along a single track road beyond the village is the Brough.

RAMBLING RIDDLE

Standing on a one-way street were two policemen looking for drivers breaking traffic laws. A taxi-driver was going the wrong way down the street, but the officers did nothing. Why?
Answer on page 153.

WALKING WORDS

Unable to resist the sun, so I caught the ten train and walked across the meadow (buttercups, forget-me-nots, ragged robins) to the Dipper stream and the ivy bridge. Read ardently in Geology till twelve. Then took off my boots and socks, and waded underneath the right arch of the bridge in deep water, and eventually sat on a dry stone at the top of the masonry just where the water drops into the green salmon pool in a solid bar. Next I wandered upstream to a big slab of rock tilted at a comfortable angle. I lay flat on this with my nether extremities in water up to my knees. The sun bathed my face and dragon flies chased up and down intent on murder. But I cared not a tinker's Demetrius about Nature red in tooth and claw. I was quite satisfied with Nature under a June sun in the cool atmosphere of a Dipper stream. I lay on the slab completely relaxed, and the cool water ran strongly between my toes. Surely I was never again going to be miserable. The voices of children playing in the wood made me extra happy. For these were fairy voices ringing through enchanted woods.
The Journal of a Disappointed Man, WNP Barbellion

QUOTE UNQUOTE

Part of the pleasure of any kind of walking for me is the very idea of going somewhere – by foot.
RUTH RUDNER,
writer

WHAT MEMBERS OF THE RAMBLERS' ASSOCIATION GET

Subscription to **walk** magazine, published four times a year.

Free *Rambler's Yearbook and Accommodation Guide*, packed with useful information.

Discretionary discounts in outdoor clothing stores.

Membership of a local walking group, a chance to meet new people and find out more about local walking routes.

You can join the Ramblers' Association online by credit or debit card (secure payment system) at www.ramblers.org.uk, by post with cheque, postal order or direct debit at The Ramblers' Association, FREEPOST SW15, London SE1 7BR, or call 020 7339 8500.

PLAY FAIR

It is against the law in Winnatka, Illinois to take your shoes off in a theatre if you have smelly feet.

10 OTHER WAYS OF GOING FOR A WALK

Spanish	el caminar/andar
German	gehen, Spazieren
Italian	camminare
French	marcher, randonner
Arabic	ÇáäÔí
Portuguese	Andar
Dutch	Lopen, wandelen
Norwegian	Gåing
Hungarian	gyaloglás, séta
Latin	pedes

SEXUAL PLEASURES THAT WALKERS MIGHT ENJOY

Dendrophilia is arousal by trees. Trees were symbols of fertility to some ancient religions, and men on certain holy days would go into the fields and have sex with them. Sex with a tree outside a holy day was frowned on, however. Stories exist of men from South American peoples who have used treeholes and clusters of leaves to have sex with, and who were distraught when they were discovered and their loved ones hacked down.

A fly on your nose, you slap and it goes;
If it comes back again, it will bring a good rain

Insects are susceptible to humidity, and will settle as a rainbelt approaches. This same rationale can be applied to the saying:

'When cows slap their sides with their tails, it is a sign of rain,'
as cattle (and horses) are greatly annoyed by flies during humid weather.

THE HIGHER THE HEEL, THE FURTHER THE FALL

Walking can be a dangerous pursuit, and not just when you're navigating a mountainous pathway. In more urban environments high fashion has brought us high shoes. And with high shoes have come some spectacular accidents.

The most famous is probably Naomi Campbell falling from her stilettos on the catwalk. The 8 inch heels by Vivienne Westwood proved to be too much for the supermodel and she went down both in stature and in fashion history.

Another celebrity to become a literal fashion victim is Emma Bunton who badly twisted her ankle after falling off her Spice Girl trademark platform trainers.

And where celebs walk, plebs will follow. Every year in Britain more than 220,000 people are admitted to casualty with injuries caused directly by what they're wearing on their feet.

Perhaps the most worrying story though is that of a Japanese nursery school teacher who fell off her shoes, cracked her skull and died of her injuries. Not to mention a spate of auto deaths resulting from women wearing ultra-high platforms who found it impossible to detect the difference between the brake and the accelerator through the 8 inches of shoe beneath their feet. This led to a call from safety bodies in the UK to include a health warning on platform shoes and even to perhaps include a kite mark to protect people from their footwear.

WHAT HAVE THE RAMBLERS EVER DONE FOR US?

The Ramblers' Association makes walking a safe and enjoyable activity by clearing blocked footpaths, building stiles and waymarking routes.

6 PLANTS THAT DON'T MAKE
FOR GOOD EATIN'

Bracken
Acute poisoning from these ferns is unlikely, due to their unpalatable taste although their crunchy tips are sometimes enjoyed as a salad vegetable. Eating bracken is not advisable however, as they do contain cyanide and have carcinogenic spores.

Foxglove
The sap, flowers, seeds and especially the leaves of foxgloves are poisonous. The leaves can be easily mistaken for those of the comfrey plant, which are traditionally used for brewing tea. The two can be distinguished however, as Foxgloves have finely toothed leaves, while the leaves of the comfrey plant are smooth.

Hemlock
All parts of the plant containing the yellow, oily sap are poisonous, especially the leaves. Consumption can cause depression of the nervous system and paralysis, leading to death. It is often mistaken for caraway but can be easily identified through its unpleasant odour, which is said to resemble that of mice.

Horse Chestnut
Although all parts of the horse chestnut are poisonous, the fruit, often mistaken for those of the sweet chestnut, cause the most problems. Horse chestnut poisoning is rarely fatal, but includes vomiting and disorientation.

Yew
The seeds and the leaves of the yew can be fatally poisonous, containing a strong concentration of caffeine. Care should be taken to ensure children steer clear of the attractive red berries.

Deadly Nightshade
Despite its name, deadly nightshade is very rarely fatal, even if eaten in large quantities. The berries can cause poisoning however, and so should be kept from children who are often attracted to the brightly coloured berries. The plant is easily recognisable with distinctive purple and yellow flowers and green or bright red berries.

HOLY WALKS

Titicaca is situated by the world's highest lake, 3,810 metres above sea level in Bolivia. Two islands – the islands of the sun and the moon – have been pilgrimage sites for centuries and a pilgrimage route has recently been discovered, dating as far back as 500BC.

MEASURE FOR PLEASURE

All you ever wanted to know about pedometers but couldn't be bothered to ask.

Pedometers measure the distance walked or run between two points by counting the number of steps taken, so you have to know your average stride length to calculate the distance covered.

Although mainly used now as a walking or running aid, pedometers have been used in the past as an aid to cartographers. Although they have been around for many years the modern invention is credited to Thomas Jefferson (1743–1826).

The principle behind the pedometer is a pendulum mechanism that moves with each detected 'gravity' shock to the mechanism, in other words, every time a step is taken. Then the mechanism counts these pulses and electronically multiplies the count by the pre-programmed step length.

For a pedometer to work, every step must be firm enough to be felt and must be close to the pre-programmed stride length.

HOW TO WALK LIKE AN EGYPTIAN

Egyptian hieroglyphics for 'walk'

4 UNUSUAL GAITS

Propulsive gait (characterised by a stooped, rigid posture, with the head and neck bent forward).

Scissors gait (characterised by legs flexed slightly at the hips and knees, giving the appearance of crouching, with the knees and thighs hitting or crossing in a scissors-like movement).

Steppage gait (characterised by foot drop where the foot hangs with the toes pointing down, causing the toes to scrape the ground while walking).

Waddling gait (characterised by a distinctive duck-like walk that may appear in childhood or later in life).

BENCH MARKED

In 1992, benches were nearly banned in a Welsh national park because walkers complained that they were depressing and ruined their days out. The Pembrokeshire Coast National Park authority had to hold a vote on whether to stop allowing people to put plaques in memory of friends and relatives on benches.

More than 70 such benches are dotted along the spectacular, 186-mile coastal path and 25 buildings also have the small memorials. 'Ramblers are saying it is becoming too morbid,' said Gordon Cawood, chairman of the park authority. 'But people put them there because it's supposed to be a memory of happy times. I think that's nice.'

QUOTE UNQUOTE

Jog on, jog on, the footpath way
And merrily hent the stile-a:
A merry heart goes all the day,
Your sad tires in a mile-a.
WILLIAM SHAKESPEARE, from *A Winter's Tale*

JOBS' WORTH

Walking trips to the English countryside support between 180,000 and 245,000 full-time jobs, according to *The Economic and Social Value of Walking in England*, The Ramblers' Association, 2003.

THIS LITTLE PIGGY...

Not everyone has 10 fingers and toes. A congenital foot condition called polydactyly occurs 1 in 1,000 births giving the child more than five toes. It is more likely to occur where there are other cases in the family. Anne Boleyn apparently had 6 fingers and toes.

Syndactyly, the webbing of fingers or toes, is another congenital condition that occurs 1 in 2,000 births. Webbing is also a hereditary condition and is more likely to occur in men than in women. Toes can be partially fused or fused along the whole length. The fusion can be simple where the toes are only connected by skin or it can be complicated with shared bone, nerves or vessels. Normally, during pregnancy as the fetus is forming the appendages, the cells in the area between the digits are programmed to 'die off'. When people have syndactyly or polydactyly this does not happen and the flesh remains connected. Both names are derived from the Greek dactylos meaning finger, while poly means many and syn means together.

MAD FOR WALKING

During the 18th and 19th centuries, pedestrianism was a popular spectator sport. One of its most noted practitioners was Capt Robert Barclay Allardice, known as 'The Celebrated Pedestrian'.

Born in 1860, an Englishwoman from Brooklyn, Ada Anderson, was one of the earliest female pedestrians. Anderson built on Barclay's most famous stunt – where he walked 1,000 miles in 1,000 hours – and in 1878 walked a quarter-mile in each quarter-hour over the 1,000 hours – that is, over the course of a month. During that month, she slept for no more than ten minutes at a time. Her efforts were justified, however, when on completing the challenge she won $10,000. And she gained celebrity to boot – thousands of people paid up to $1 each to see the walk. Her achievements encouraged many other nineteenth-century women to follow – quite literally – in her footsteps.

5 SURE SIGNS OF RAIN

You know it's going to rain when...

...pine cone needles become pliable which means they are absorbing moisture.

...birds are hanging around near to the ground. The low air pressure of a storm keeps insects low where consequently the birds feed.

...cows bunch together and huddle into a sheltered valley. If they only shelter under a tree however, the storm will only be short.

...cows are lying down. They can sense it is going to rain due to the electricity in the air so are getting a dry patch while they can!

...you notice the smell of rain. This is because wet air transmits smells of tree and soil oils more strongly when humidity is high.

OSTRICH MAULS HIKER

This strange incident from the Saldanha Bay guest farm shows that Britain's lack of exotic fauna might well be a blessing to walkers. In September 1998 a group of South African hikers who were staying at the farm were suddenly targeted by an ostrich, its wings spread in an aggressive posture. For 40 minutes, one of the male members of the group was kicked and jumped on by the huge bird. The ostrich left him on the ground needing 12 stitches where its claw had torn his cheek open.

MUSHROOM MAGIC

Types of edible fungi you might want to chomp on as you wander around the world.

A word of caution – bring a good guide book!

Common Name	Latin Name
Enoki, Golden mushroom	*Flammulina velutipes*
Horse mushroom	*Agaricus arvensis*
Lion's mane	*Hericium erinaceum*
Braunkappe, Wine Cap	*Stropharia rugosoannulata*
Shiitake	*Lentinula edodes*
Straw mushroom	*Volvariella volvacea*
Wood blewit, Blewit	*Lepista nuda*
Black truffle	*Tuber melanosporum* or *aestivum*
Chanterelle, Girolle	*Cantharellus cibarius*
Autumn Chanterelle	*Craterellus tubaeformis,*
Mousseron	*Marasmius oreades*
Morille, Morel	*Morchella esculenta*
Pied de mouton	*Hydnum repandum*
St George's Mushroom	*Calocybe gambosa*
Trompette des morts	*Craterellus cornucopioides*

QUOTE UNQUOTE

Many people will walk in and out of your life but only true friends will leave footprints in your heart
ELEANOR ROOSEVELT,
stateswoman

HOW TO TIE LACES

1. Take one shoelace in one hand, the second lace in the other and hold both of them straight up. Then crisscross the laces over each other to make a big X.
2. Fold one lace over the other and pull that lace through the bottom half of the X; then pull both of the laces tight until they lie nice and flat against the shoe.
3. Make two loops, one with each shoelace.
4. Make an X with the loops, holding the centre of the X in place with your thumb and finger.
5. Fold one loop over the other (as you did with the first X) and pull that loop through the bottom half of the X. Now pull both loops tight through the hole to form a bow.
6. Step out with confidence.

WHO'S THAT WALKING ACROSS THE ROAD
WITH JOHN, GEORGE AND RINGO?

There is a theory that Paul McCartney is dead. He was supposedly killed in a car crash in 1966 and a look-a-like brought was in to cover up the death so that the Beatles could keep going. It is not clear where this theory originated but clues in the Beatles' album covers have been used by conspiracists to prove the 'truth' of the theory. The *Abbey Road* (released 26 September 1969) album cover which shows the group walking across a zebra crossing has thrown up plenty of discussion points that are still bandied about in the appropriate conspiracy circles:

In the procession, John represents the preacher (or god) as he is dressed in white, Ringo represents a pall bearer or undertaker, Paul is the deceased and George is the gravedigger.

Paul is walking bare foot and has his eyes closed, indicative of a corpse.

Paul is out of step with the others, his right foot is forward where the others are leading with their left foot.

A Volkswagen has a licence plate that says '28 IF'. At the album's release, Paul would have been 28 if he were alive.

The licence plate is then followed by LMW, representing Linda McCartney Weeps.

Paul is holding a cigarette in his right hand despite the fact that he is left-handed, suggesting that this man was in fact the replacement and not the real Paul.

There is a police vehicle parked to the right in the photograph.

The car in the background is headed directly at Paul.

RAMBLING RIDDLE

A man walks into a bar and asks for a glass of water. The barman draws a gun on him. The man thanks him, and leaves the bar without drinking the water. Why?
Answer on page 153.

HOLY WALKS

Varanasi, on the River Ganges in India is considered home to the Indian God Shiva. People lucky enough to die in Varanasi are considered privileged enough to be liberated from the cycle of life and death and thousands journey to the city to end their days.

The others pretended not to hear as, for the ninth time, Algy did his 'if-this-is-a-conducted-ramble-then-here's-my-baton' joke.

JACANA? NO, SHE WENT OF HER OWN ACCORD

The jacana is a southern hemisphere bird that walks across lilypads in search of snacks. To even its weight out across as large a surface as possible to avoid sinking, its toes are up to 10cm long. These are the longest toes of any bird in proportion to its size.

THE WALKER'S FAVOURITE FOOD

In a recent BBC survey sandwiches were voted as the nation's favourite outdoor food ahead of hotdogs and steak (which are, of course, perhaps not so good for walkers).

The sandwich was invented by John Montagu, the 4th Earl of Sandwich. The story goes that he was a gambler and wanted a meal he could eat while holding his cards.

The ham sandwich is the most popular sandwich in the US.

The biggest sandwich eaters in Europe are the French, behind the British.

Mamas and Papas star Cass Elliot died when she choked on a sandwich in 1974. British Sandwich Week was launched in 1998.

Fascinatingly enough, there is a British Sandwich Association, founded in January 1990.

The aims of The British Sandwich Association are:

• To safeguard the integrity of the sandwich industry by setting technical standards for sandwich making and by encouraging improvement in the industry.
• To promote excellence and innovation in sandwich making.
• To provide a source of information for the industry.
• To promote the consumption of sandwiches.
• To provide a collective voice for all those involved in making, distributing and retailing sandwiches and to represent the views of the industry.

WALK THIS WAY

'The Ministry of Silly Walks' is a sketch from Monty Python's Flying Circus, episode 14. This episode was recorded on 9 July 1970 and aired on 15 September 1970. The sketch was also shortened and performed during Monty Python Live at the Hollywood Bowl.

The sketch involves John Cleese as the Minister of Silly Walks being presented with a 'walk in progress' by one Mr Pudney (Michael Palin). Sadly for Mr Pudney's hopes, the walk turns out to be not that silly after all.

However, this memorable sketch has cast a long shadow: one of the reasons the government has consistently shied clear of implementing a sensible strategy to promote more walking and improve conditions for pedestrians is undoubtedly the fear of being ridiculed by the media for setting up a Ministry of Silly Walks.

THOSE FIRST STEPS

Humans learn to walk anywhere between seven and 16 months unlike most animals that can walk from birth.

Why humans can't walk from birth

• They do not have strong enough neck muscles to hold up their heads

• They do not have strong enough leg muscles to hold up and balance the body

• They do not have strong enough eye muscle control to open their eyelids and see objects in their way

When babies start to walk...

• They start to take weight on their feet and appear to have no arch due mainly to a pad of fat under the foot. By 4 or 5 years the arch has developed.

• Many babies' legs have a naturally bowed or bandy appearance

• They often walk with their legs wide apart for balance

• They have to use trial and error and have to learn to walk without using language

• They have to learn to balance in many positions and learn to shift their weight

Who'd be a baby!

HOLY WALKS

According to legend a finger of an Indian Goddess fell to the earth at Kalighat, in Calcutta, India. A temple grew out of the story and today thousands visit the shrine where a goat is sacrificed daily and free food is given out to the poor.

QUOTE UNQUOTE

Everywhere is within walking distance if you have the time.
STEVEN WRIGHT, comedian

THEY MUST BE QUACKERS

Strongman competitions have become very popular in many countries, not least the US, Canada and Iceland. During the tournaments, these men of steel, sinew and stamina put themselves through a series of trials that normal folk wouldn't even consider attempting even in teams of ten. One of the events is the duck walk, in which contestants waddle for a few yards carrying a 440lb weight between their legs. Sounds tough enough, but then true masochism takes over: they carry the weight up a flight of steps.

3 FAMOUS NURSERY RHYMES TO INTRODUCE THE CONCEPT OF WALKING TO HAPPY CHILDREN EVERYWHERE

Jack and Jill
Went up the hill
To fetch a pail of water.
Jack fell down
And broke his crown
And Jill came tumbling after.

Up Jack got
And home did trot
As fast as he could caper
He went to bed
To mend his head
With vinegar and brown paper.

There was a crooked man
Who walked a crooked mile.
He found a crooked sixpence
Upon a crooked stile.
He bought a crooked cat
Which caught a crooked mouse,
And they all lived together
In a little crooked house.

Oh, the grand old Duke of York,
He had ten thousand men;
He marched them up to the top of the hill,
And he marched them down again.

And, when they were up they were up;
And when they were down they were down.
And when they were only halfway up,
They were neither up nor down.

QUOTE UNQUOTE

One must always have one's boots on and be ready to go
MICHEL DE MONTAIGNE,
essayist

The story of Captain Robert Falcon Scott's final walk in 1912 is well known. Having been beaten to the South pole by Norwegian rival Roald Amundsen (who had the cheek to be dragged there by teams of dogs, unlike the stiff-upper-lipped Scott, who insisted on walking every step of the way), he and his four men turned for home. Petty Officer Edgar Evans died on the way back, as did Captain Oates, who famously walked out of the tent one night – his birthday – announcing that he 'was just going outside, and may be some time'. Scott, Lt 'Birdie' Bowers and Dr Edward Wilson trudged on, dying about a dozen miles short of One Ton Depot, where food and fuel awaited them.

Scott's walk may be the most celebrated, but the overall expedition involved several other extraordinary feats on foot, which are less well-known perhaps because they were more successful. After all, the English have always loved heroic failures.

* Many men set off in Scott's party to support the push for the pole, turning back in small groups at various stages of the route. Eventually the final three – the last men to see Scott's polar party alive – turned back. They were Lt 'Teddy' Evans, PO Tom Crean, and PO William Lashly. On the way back to base camp, Lt Evans fell badly ill with scurvy. He could no longer walk. Crean and Lashly dragged him for several miles on the sledge, but he had become a burden. They pitched a tent, and while Lashly stayed with the invalid, Crean set off on the final 35 miles to get help. He wandered through a raging blizzard accompanied by nothing but two chocolate bars and three biscuits. He made it, and the rescue party saved both Evans and Lashly. Upon his arrival at base camp, Crean was given a tot of brandy and some porridge, and promptly threw up. 'That's the first time in my life that ever it happened, and it was the brandy that did it,' said the rugged County Kerry man who upon his return to Ireland was to open a pub.

* A few months before the polar push, three members of Scott's party set off on a scientific expedition to discover how Emperor penguin eggs survived the harsh Antarctic weather. The three – Bowers, Wilson and Apsley Cherry-Garrard – hauled their sledge for 60 miles in freezing temperatures, lost their tent and lay huddled in sleeping bags for two days, sleepwalked in their own tracks, and finally made it back to camp with a cargo of eggs. Cherry-Garrard wrote up the tale a few years later as *The Worst Journey in the World*.

'If you march your Winter Journeys you will have your reward,' he wrote, 'so long as all you want is a penguin's egg'.

RAMBLING RIDDLE

A man walks 10 miles south, 10 miles east, and 10 miles north to arrive back at his starting point. A bear follows him. What colour is it?
Answer on page 153.

THE DEVIL STEPS OUT

The week in mid-January 1909 has long haunted the residents of Burlington, New Jersey, USA. It was the week that the Jersey Devil walked, in one night alone, leaving its prints in the snow across back gardens, across rooftops, up trees and out into open fields where they disappeared. A posse of dogs refused to track it.

The Jersey Devil has been described as being 'about three feet and a half high, with a head like a collie dog and a face like a horse. It has a long neck, wings about two feet long, its back legs are like those of a crane, and it has horse's hooves.' Legend has it that the Devil was born to a Mrs Shrouds of Leeds Point, New Jersey, some time in the 18th century. Some say that the mother was so cursed because, with 12 children already eating their way through house and home, she declared that a 13th could only be a devil. Others have it that the beast was the lovechild of her illicit dalliances with a British soldier.

Whatever its origins, the Jersey Devil became one of the most sighted cryptozoological creatures of the 19th century, before saving its best appearances for the 20th century, and in particular that week in 1909.

Since that date, unusual tracks have continued to be found in the area, often nearby the half-eaten corpse of a duck, goat or dog.

WHY WALK WHEN YOU CAN TRAVELATE?

If you can't be bothered to walk, use a travelator. Travelators are escalators that also carry you along on the flat. The longest in the world is the 800-metre moving walkway on Hong Kong island, which basks under the prosaic title of Central-Mid-Levels Escalator and Walkway System.

QUOTE UNQUOTE

If you would grow great and stately, you must try to walk sedately.
ROBERT LOUIS STEVENSON,
novelist

Locomotion research was the key to military success in the 18th and 19th centuries.

Marching theory treated a regiment as a mechanical system, carefully quantifying the length and cadence of each soldier's step and the movement of bodies through space.

The first musket drills were developed by the Dutch in the late 16th century, but they reached an apex of precision among the Prussians of the mid-18th century. On the basis of battlefield observations, Frederick the Great's soldiers were taught to stand erect yet relaxed and to swing their legs stiffly as they marched. To synchronise their movements they stamped their heels on the ground and clapped their gun barrels in unison, while drill sergeants timed their steps with stopwatches.

Prussian martinets were a military wonder. In 1763, when the Prussians defeated France and its allies in the Seven Years' War, they owed their triumph, in part, to better walking. As a result, the single-mindedness and discipline of military drills became a blueprint for everything from manliness to philosophy to political authority in Prussia.

Beginning in the 1820s, Eduard, Wilhelm and Ernst Heinrich Weber, three German brothers with backgrounds in physiology, anatomy and mechanics, established the world's first movement laboratory. The Webers used Hanoverian soldiers as subjects, but they tried to make the soldiers forget their training: they wanted to study natural walking, not marching. In their 1836 book, *Mechanics of the Human Walking Apparatus*, the Webers described the undulations of the spine, the inclination of the pelvis and the effects of wind and gravity on the body. Their conclusion – that the body's natural gait is more efficient than marching in most situations – brought walking science full circle.

Locomotion research has gradually faded to the background, into biomechanics and orthopedics labs, and is no longer destined to turn the tides of war.

QUOTE UNQUOTE

Me thinks that the moment my legs begin to move, my thoughts begin to flow.
HENRY DAVID THOREAU, naturalist and writer

IN THE FOOTSTEPS OF BUDDHA

One of the many interesting aspects of Buddhism is the tradition of Buddha footprints. Footprints are just one sign of the presence of the Buddha – the others being the bodhi tree, an umbrella, a throne, and the dharmachakra or wheel of the Law.

Tradition holds that the Buddha (Gotama), or an incarnation known as 'the future buddha' (Metreya) left these behind to guide us to enlightenment. When found in nature, these relics are subjected to extreme scrutiny to ensure they have all the right signs, then they become places of worship.

Footprints of the Buddha exist in Afghanistan, Bhutan, Cambodia, China, India, Japan, Korea, Laos, Malaysia, the Maldives, Pakistan, Singapore, Sri Lanka, Thailand and Burma. The first footprints appeared during the appatima period that started in the earliest period of Buddhism and which remained strong until the 4th century.

THE PEDESTRIAN CODE OF CONDUCT

The rules about which side of the road people drive on are clear, but there are also 'rules' that govern how pedestrians behave in relation to each other. These pedestrian rules are not usually codified in law but form a sort of 'standard practice' which many people are not even consciously aware of until they travel to a country with a different standard practice and end up bumping into the locals.

Keep right:
Keeping right is the normal practice in the US and Canada.
France also keeps to the right.
Pedestrians in Taiwan keep right.

Keep left:
People in Japan keep left when walking.
There is a vague tendency to keep left in Australia and New Zealand.
In Hong Kong there is also a slight tendency to walk on the left.

No preference: The United Kingdom seems not to have a preference as to which side of the path to use when walking.

This doesn't mean that the British bump into each other. They don't tend to use single-file traffic, but they still manage to negotiate their way effectively using body language, eye contact, and other cues to signal their intentions and notice others' intentions.

MILITARY STRIDES AND HOW TO DO THEM

Speed	Steps per minute	Distance per minute	Step Length
Slow	75	62 yds 18 ins	30"
Quick	110	91 yds 24 ins	30"
Double	150	150 yds	36"
Side	Quick Time	Varies	10"
Stepping Out	Slow or quick time	Varies	33"
Stepping Short	Slow or quick time	Varies	10"

2 TOP TESTED TIPS

A plain silk shawl (or a 4'/120cm silk square for men) makes an ultra-light/compact head/body insulator, or an under-blanket for cold camps/draughty dorms.

A pint-size plastic milk bottle (with top of course) makes a light, leak/spill-proof container for gathering wild fruits like blackberries. Hook it on your little finger to leave the rest of the fingers free to gather/hold down briars.

ANIMAL MAGIC

The placement of a donkey's eyes in its head enables it to see all four of its feet.

Newfoundland dogs are strong swimmers thanks to their webbed feet.

Mosquitoes prefer biting people with smelly feet.

Polar bears are the only mammals with hair on the soles of their feet.

A tiger's paw prints are called pug marks.

Butterflies taste with their back feet.

Cats step with both left legs, then both right legs, when they walk or run. The only other animals to do this are the giraffe and the camel. The domestic cat is also the only species able to hold its tail vertically while walking. Wild cats hold their tail horizontally or tucked between their legs.

40% of all cats are ambidextrous.
The other 60% are either right- or left-pawed.

Elephants walk on tip-toe because the back part of their foot is made of fat and no bone.

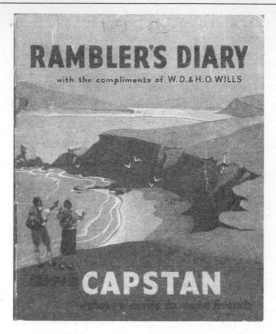

In 1950, cigarette makers WD & HO Wills published a small
Rambler's Diary. In amongst titbits of information on what natural
delights each month might offer, they published the following advice:
*Fainting: Lay the patient down with the head low and the legs
raised. Loosen tight clothing. In hot weather make sure the patient is
not overheated. In cold weather keep him warm – it is especially
important to have something underneath the patient to protect him
from the coldness of the ground.*
*Whatever happens, always try to keep calm. Smoke a Capstan or a
Woodbine: it will help you.*

QUOTE UNQUOTE

*A vigorous five-mile walk will do more good for an unhappy
but otherwise healthy adult than all the medicine and psychology
in the world*
PAUL DUDLEY WHITE, cardiologist

RED WALKERS

Recent research is suggesting that Chairman Mao Zedong's famous Long March across China was a lot shorter than has been claimed by the Chinese Communist Party. The trek was undertaken in 1934 by the Red Army and has traditionally been fixed at 7,500 miles, taking a year to complete. 100,000 soldiers and party leaders walked through 11 provinces, 18 mountain ranges and 24 rivers and as a result Mao gained unchallenged command of the Communist Party. Only 28,000 marchers reached the end. However, a recent retracing of the route (by just two men) has found that the journey was actually about 2,500 miles shorter than the traditional claims.

THE NUMBER OF STEPS UP TO VARIOUS TOWERS

Eiffel Tower	2731
Empire State Building	1860
CN Tower	2579
Menara Tower, Kuala Lumpur, Malaysia	1850
Leaning Tower of Pisa	294

THE ELEPHANT MAN

Hannibal was a Carthaginian general and leader of a famous march across the Alps. When the Second Punic War between Rome and Carthage broke out in 218 BC, Hannibal set off from Carthage in Spain and marched with thousands of soldiers and even elephants. The 40,000 soldiers marched across the Pyrenees and then later across the Alps but the trip had a devastating effect on the group and it is thought that 26,000 soldiers were lost through exposure, desertion, accidents and resistance from mountain tribes, and most of the elephants died. However, the crossing marked the first crossing of the Alps by a co-ordinated army and was an astonishing distance covered by a huge group of men.

WALKING WORDS

Like one that on a lonesome road
Doth walk in fear and dread
And having once turned round walks on
And turns no more his head
Because he knows, a frightful fiend
Doth close behind him tread
Samuel Taylor Coleridge, *The Rime of the Ancient Mariner*

150 *Amount, in thousands of dollars, for which Charlie Chaplin insured his feet in the 1920s*

Walked 3.7 miles back and forth to the coffee machine

Wore odd socks on 17 different days

Bought five new pairs of shoes, and took one pair back

Developed seven blisters, three of which were on their feet

Bought a thermos flask to find out how it worked but broke it

Ate 476 sandwiches, of which chicken mayonnaise was the most popular, but cheese and ham made a good showing

Visited 1,876 websites without moving

Paced around in circles an average 6.32 times a day

Found out what urtication is, but decided not to try it

Borrowed 89 walking books from libraries, and lost 11

Sleepwalked four times, once during office hours

Tried tightrope walking between two desks, which explains the broken thermos

Please note that although every effort has been made to ensure accuracy in this book, the above statistics may be the result of rambling minds.

Before you criticise someone,
walk a mile in his shoes.
Then when you do criticise that person,
you'll be a mile away and have his shoes!

Frieda Norris, writer

The answers. As if you needed them.

P12.   Halfway. After he gets halfway, he's walking out of the forest

P20.   A human being. A toddler crawls, an adult walks, and the elderly uses a walking stick

P26.   Side

P34.   As the dog was always running twice as fast as Charlotte, who travelled 10 miles, then the dog must have run 20 miles

P46.   Moon

P52.   Walk

P60.   Walking back to happiness (to = two)

P70.   Andrew. 'He tipped his hat and drew his cane'

P77.   Fork in the road

P87.   High King in the woods = hiking in the woods

P90.   Ramble and Amble

P105. Walk away from it

P108. One step forward, two steps back

P114. The rate of reproduction would be faster than the speed of the walking line

P120. Walk on the wild side

P124. Man

P131. The taxi driver was walking at the time and not driving his cab, therefore breaking no traffic laws

P139. He wanted the water to cure his hiccoughs. The barman drew his gun to give him the fright he needed to do the job instead

P145. White. He starts at the North Pole

*All paths lead nowhere, so it is important
to choose a path that has heart.*

Carlos Castaneda, writer

ACKNOWLEDGEMENTS

We gratefully acknowledge permission to reprint extracts of copyright material in this book from the following authors, publishers and executors:

Just So Stories by Rudyard Kipling by permission of A P Watt Ltd on behalf of the National Trust for places of historic interest or natural beauty

The Way Through the Woods by Rudyard Kipling by permission of A P Watt Ltd on behalf of the National Trust for places of historic interest or natural beauty

A Literary Pilgrim in England by Edward Thomas by kind permission of Myfanwy Thomas

In Pursuit of Spring by Edward Thomas by kind permission of Myfanwy Thomas

Agnes Grey by Anne Bronte by kind permission of the Bronte Parsonage Museum

Into the Heart of Borneo reprinted by permission of PFD on behalf of Redmond O'Hanlon

Between the Woods and the Water by Patrick Leigh Fermor by kind permission of John Murray Publishers

The Oldest Road, by J R L Anderson published by Whittet Books

The Mill on the Floss by George Eliot by kind permission of Jonathan Ouvry

The Color Purple by Alice Walker published by the Women's Press, by permission of David Higham Associates

Walking in England by Geoffrey Trease by kind permission of David Higham Associates

Every effort has been made to contact copyright holders. We apologise for any unintentional errors or omissions.

WALKING NOTES, JOTTINGS, IDEAS AND DOODLES

WALKING NOTES, JOTTINGS, IDEAS AND DOODLES

The Walker's Companion is published by
Think Books, part of Think Publishing, the UK's
leading environmental publisher

Working towards a more sustainable future

Environmental perceptions are changing in Britain.
Where once the ecologist or conservationist was seen as a breed
apart, in today's post-modern age environmental concerns are
fitting into our daily lives. Recycling, charitable donations and
organic farming are becoming part of the British culture, and
millions of people are joining in.

These people are often called green consumers but, in reality,
most of them are like you or me: they want the right to take
walks in the countryside, to eat unpolluted food, to visit
unspoilt regions of the world, and to ensure that their children
can enjoy these pleasures in the years to come. We like to call
them, and indeed ourselves, conscientious consumers.

Think Publishing firmly believes that our group is growing every
day and that protection and understanding of the world around
us should be built in to what we all do.

Through the magazines and books that we publish, we
constantly try to develop this ethos.

Tilly Boulter, Director
Think Publishing
020 8962 3020
tilly@thinkpublishing.co.uk
www.thinkpublishing.co.uk
November 2003

THINK
BOOKS

OTHER TITLES AVAILABLE FROM THINK BOOKS

WILDLIFE WALKS
Great Days Out at Over 500 of the UK's Top Nature Reserves
Wildlife Walks is the perfect guide for nature-lovers and families who are planning a great day out across the UK. Covering over 500 of The Wildlife Trusts' nature reserves, and including over 400 original colour maps, illustrations and photographs, Wildlife Walks provides the key to exploring these open spaces and the creatures great and small that inhabit them. 450pp. 2003.
£9.99

GO M.A.D.! 2 OVER 500 DAILY WAYS TO SAVE THE PLANET
Go Make a Difference! 2 is a must-have for every home. Here are over 500 easy and practical tips that everyone can easily adopt to be more environmentally responsible. The first edition of Go MAD! has already sold 45,000 copies nationwide. Go MAD! 2 has revised and extended the original content, while retaining the handy pocket format. So, whether you want to throw a green party that doesn't cost the earth, or just want to find alternatives to all those chemicals in your shed, now you can Go Make A Difference! 274pp. 2003.
£6.99

3 easy ways to order your copies today
PHONE Call the order hotline on 0870 010 9700 (Mon–Fri, 9-5, Sat 9-midday) with your credit card details.
ON-LINE Order on-line at www.wildlifebooks.co.uk with your credit card details.
POST Send a cheque for the book price plus £1.99 post and packing for the first book and 25p per book for any further books, made payable to Think Publishing, to: Think Publishing, The Pall Mall Deposit, 124-128 Barlby Road, London W10 6BL, with your name and address written clearly on the back.

ALL BOOKS ALSO AVAILABLE IN BOOKSHOPS NATIONWIDE